HEALTHY MEALS FOR BUSY PEOPLE

LEAH ITSINES

HEALTHY MEALS FOR BUSY PEOPLE

100 recipes
for every kind of busy

murdoch books
Sydney | London

CONTENTS

Hi, thank you for picking me up!

Hello my friend, how are you feeling? Tired? Busy? Like you have a never-ending to-do list and you're wondering how you're going to manage it all PLUS get the laundry done (without that sneaky re-spin-because-you're-not-ready-to-hang-it-out)? Trust me, I hear you. And I want to reassure you that everyone feels like this at times, whether they show it or not.

I think we can all agree that no matter where you are in life, there will always be stages when you feel extra busy and extra overwhelmed. And guess what we do when this happens? We put ourselves last. Our health, our nutrition, our wellbeing – they all take a back seat, which sucks. And that's what I'm trying to change with this book.

My philosophy when it comes to food is that we need to have a balance – no matter what your goals are. I come from a big Greek family, and we're all about fresh, delicious food that is made with love. As a mum of two, I understand that we can't always be cooking all day like our grandparents might have; we have too much on for that. My goal is to provide tips, tricks and a collection of foolproof recipes that are purpose-built to be easy, low-effort and nutritious, so you can nourish yourself even on your most hectic days. This is modern cooking: simple recipes, designed so that you can make them in bulk, prep ahead, or freeze them to give you a little bit of ease come mealtime. So, let's eat!

You're doing great.

Leah x

MANAGING YOUR BUSY

Before we get into the food, I want to give you a little pep talk from Mama Leah. Before I had kids, one thing I heard *a lot* was 'You don't know what busy is until you have kids.' Now, I get it – it's a dream come true if I can leave the house without shouting 'Where are your shoes?' or 'Yes, you can have a lollipop if you just get in the car!'. The goalposts move in every era of life, so defining YOUR busy is really important.

WHAT MAKES YOU FEEL BUSY?

Everyone has their own definition of what makes them feel busy, overwhelmed, stressed, etc. Whether it be work, kids, health, family, friends – any or all of these can contribute to your mountain, so I want to reiterate here that your circumstances are unique, and it's important to focus on YOU and not anyone else.

FOCUS ON YOU

In a world where we are living on our phones and everything seems to be a highlight reel of other people's lives, it's so important to focus on yourself, no matter how hard that might be. Many people are in a different life stage from you, so your priorities might be completely different. You may find yourself wondering 'How do they do it all when I feel I can't?' but the reality is, you don't know their story or what goes on behind the scenes. It's all too easy to watch from a surface-level perspective and question yourself.

AN IMPORTANT QUESTION TO ASK YOURSELF

Instead of 'What are they doing that I can do too?', ask yourself 'What do *I* want right now? Which of my needs have to be met to make myself feel good?'

Remember, it's *your* busy - no one else's.

WHAT NEEDS TO BE TRUE

In my 'non' busy (aka doomscroll!) time, I recently came across Dr John Delony, a psychologist with a podcast on YouTube. One of the questions he asks of people is along the lines of 'What things need to be true in your home for you to be less (insert how you're feeling)?'. I think this is a GREAT question to ask yourself in relation to feeling overwhelmed.

What needs to be true? Do you need to clean the dishes before bed so you wake up with a clean house? Do you need to make time for yourself? Do you need to ask for help or delegate if possible? So many questions, and only you can answer for yourself, but it is important to know what needs to be true, so you're able to start taking baby steps towards making that happen.

CREATE YOUR NON-NEGOTIABLES

Once you have some answers to the question 'What needs to be true?', set some non-negotiables and do everything in your power to stick to them. For example, the non-negotiable for my day is to wake up before my little ones. It's such a simple thing, but it changes the entire aura of my day – it makes me feel less stressed and less busy because I have a moment to myself before the chaos begins.

YOU'RE BUSY NOW, BUT YOU'RE NOT BEHIND

Something powerful to remember is that you might be busy, you might feel overwhelmed with life, but you're not 'behind' anyone else. Your life, your timeline, your health, your nutrition and everything else is yours, and there is no need to rush. You've done the first great thing in picking up this book for some help, so you're already one step ahead.

BUSY TIP

Non-negotiables can be things like going to the gym, meal prepping, skincare in the morning – anything that makes you feel good!

NUTRITION TALK
Why food matters when we're busy

When life is busy, you'll need to power yourself adequately to keep up with the hectic pace. In fact, in my humble opinion, this is the most important time to focus on what's fuelling you.

ENERGY

Prepping food is often seen as a chore, and in busy times we are more likely to grab convenience foods that give us short bursts of energy, followed by inevitable crashes. These crashes can exacerbate an already stressful situation. Nutritious food should be our fuel throughout the day, to help us with decision-making, to improve our concentration, and to stabilise energy - so think of it as something you need to prioritise.

'BUSY' FOOD CAN BE REALLY SIMPLE

Though there are some days when we might have a little more free time to make elaborate meals with longer cook times (see the Got Time? I've Got You. chapter), it is absolutely okay to grab pre-made sauces from the shops to make your life easier. I've tried to keep this book simple by giving you the option to do both. If you have the time? Great, make pesto from scratch. If not, no worries - a store-bought option is absolutely fine, too.

THE RIPPLE EFFECT

When we ensure our diet is at its best (or as good as we can make it) this has a beneficial ripple effect without us even knowing it. We think more clearly, we have more energy and our mood is likely to be more positive, JUST from eating the good stuff! This isn't to say it needs to be exactly on point every day, but just making small changes (ensuring you get enough protein, drinking plenty of water, eating regularly to fuel your day) can truly make a big difference.

A PERFECT EASY WAY TO BUILD A 'BUSY' MEAL

Think of your plate broken up into sections - these are the 'pillars' that form an entire meal. Load up on veggies and protein, include some good fats and grains, and don't forget the flavour!

You can buy some of these foods in single serves (tuna, rice) or make them in bulk (salad dressings, sauces and proteins such as marinated meats that you can freeze).

Vegetables: A bag of frozen veggies is a dream come true when I need dinner on the table in minutes. Try to include a wide variety of colours when it comes to veg.

Protein: Protein keeps you full, so don't skip it! Tinned fish or beans, lentils, cooked chicken, fish, beef, or even something convenient like deli ham or barbecue chicken.

Flavours:
Even if you're busy, you don't deserve bland food! Store-bought sauces, spices and salts can really enhance a meal.

Fats:
Simple additions to meals that don't require cooking, like nuts and seeds or healthy oils.

Grain foods: Foods such as rice, quinoa, pasta and noodles keep you fuelled.

LOAD YOUR FRIDGE & PANTRY WITH THE BASICS

Having your fridge and pantry stocked with simple basics means you can whip up something quick, easy and delicious in no time. Basics are the base of every kitchen, and once you're set it becomes much easier to be motivated to explore, as things are ready to go with less stress. Here's a peek inside my fridge and pantry!

FRIDGE

- **Baby spinach** or **mixed salad leaves** – always good for a quick salad.
- **Tomatoes**, **cucumbers**, **carrots**, **capsicums** - these veggies are not only versatile but also have a longer fridge life, making them great to keep on hand week to week. I find myself always grabbing these at the farmers' markets.
- **Zucchini** and **mushrooms** - my go-tos for bulking up meals. They cook quickly, soak up flavour and can be added to almost anything (zucchini cakes, anyone?).
- **Lemons** and **limes** - simple additions that finish off meals to get that extra flavour with minimal effort.
- **Eggs** - a great, quick source of protein that you can boil in advance and have in the fridge ready for salads, breakfast on-the-go or snacks.
- **Feta** - a salty, creamy addition to salads, but also a quick one for easy breakfasts (feta eggs). I always choose feta stored in brine: it stays fresher for longer.
- **Shredded cheese** - cheese is always a good little topper, addition or flavour for quick meals such as burrito bowls, pizzas etc.
- **Sauces** – sauces like tomato, mustard, barbecue, Kewpie and mayo are all great to have on hand so you can top your meals with extra flavour.

⟶ *continued*

PANTRY

- **Tinned goods/long-life items**: things like **tinned fish, legumes, crushed tomatoes, tinned vegetables, tinned soups, chicken stocks, tomato purée, noodle packets etc.** These are all pantry winners because they are cost-effective and perfect for last-minute meals.
- **Spices**: my spice drawer has filled slowly over time, but now I'm running out of room! Start small with simple things like **salt, pepper, dried oregano, dried parsley, dried basil, garlic granules, onion powder** and **chilli powder**, and slowly build from there, based on what you love to sprinkle in!
- **Single-serve packaged snacks**: crucial to my 'mum life', because I never have both hands free! Stocking up on things like **protein bars** and **nut/trail mixes** when they're on sale is a perfect way to ensure you have something on hand for a quick grab and run out the door.
- **Oils and sauces:** olive oil is my go-to oil and I buy it in bulk when it's on sale. Classic sauces like **soy sauce, oyster sauce, fish sauce, chilli oils** and **vinegars** are essential if you want to be able to quickly whip up a meal.
- **Bulk goods**: staples like **rice, flour, breadcrumbs, sugars** and **pastas** are great to buy in bulk when on special. All of these store well and are great bases for many meals.

BUSY TIP

Take advantage of grocery delivery if available! I only recently started using delivery and it's been a lifesaver. I can order groceries in bed while the kids are sleeping and I feel so organised.

HOW YOUR FREEZER CAN HELP ON BUSY NIGHTS

When life feels busy, there's nothing better than opening the freezer to find your previous self has gifted you ready-to-go meals or containers of goodness that will cut your cooking time (and effort) in half. Think sauces, curries, lasagnes – anything that can help you get dinner on the table quicker, that's what we want to see! When you're busy, a stocked freezer can be your secret weapon.

BULK SAUCES →

Napoletana sauce, bolognese sauce, meatballs in sauce, curries and soups are some of my favourite things to make and freeze because they not only last super long, but they are so easy to take out and reheat, meaning no fuss at dinnertime. If you have time and you're cooking a recipe that can be frozen, consider doubling or tripling the ingredients and freezing the extra for when you are a little busier.

MARINATED MEATS →

This one is a total game changer! I prepare meats, fish etc. with different marinades and freeze them raw. The morning of, I pop them in the fridge to defrost. Come dinnertime, it's super easy to throw together a satisfying meal. This makes for less clean-up, and a super quick cook!

SMART PORTIONS →

I freeze most of my meals in single or double serves. This way, you can pull out only what you need and minimise wastage.

FREEZING TIMES

This is a general guide to freezing times to help keep your food fresh and safe to eat. While some items can be frozen longer, I prefer to rotate most things a little more frequently to maintain quality.

FOOD	FREEZING TIME
Soups	3 months
Vegetables	4–6 months
Raw meat/ poultry	4–6 months
Cooked meat/ poultry	2–3 months
Cooked fish	1 month
Raw fish	3 months
Muffins	1–2 months
Egg items	1–2 months
Sauces	4–6 months
Fruit	3 months
Bread, wraps, pizza bases	3–6 months
Pastries	1–2 months
Herbs in oil, etc.	1–2 months

HOW TO NOT GET OVERWHELMED BY MEAL PREP

Meal prep has been a game changer in my life. It is incredible how much time it opens up across the week and how easy it is to eat healthily when your meals are *basically* already done when you walk through the door. If you're not someone who has prepared meals before, welcome to the party! Let's break it down for you so it isn't so overwhelming.

WHAT IS MEAL PREP?

Meal prep is simply preparing meals or ingredients ahead of time. It can include meal planning, grocery shopping, cleaning out the fridge, tidying the pantry, chopping vegetables, batch cooking or preparing full meals in advance. These small actions can make a huge difference across the week.

WHAT FOODS CAN I PREP?

There are many foods that you can prep, but there are also foods I prefer to make fresh. You can prep any food that stores well in the refrigerator and keeps its taste and texture after a few days, like cooked meats, poultry or fish, cooked vegetables, grains, soups, sauces and hard raw vegetables like carrots and broccoli.

I would avoid prepping things like fruit or things that you know won't last more than a couple of hours after being prepared (i.e. nachos would go soggy in the refrigerator). If you are prepping salads, hold off adding the dressing until it is time to eat.

I DON'T HAVE TIME TO DO IT IN ONE DAY!

Meal prep is what you make it. A friend of mine who's a shiftworker prefers to have all her meals for the week prepared so she can grab and eat, or take her food to an overnight shift. I don't prep every single meal; just do what you can.

I also don't do my prep all in one day... that would be super overwhelming for most people! This is how I break it down into smaller jobs, so it feels easier on the brain.

Meal prep tasks

Friday
Meal planning and writing shopping list

Saturday
Grocery shopping or ordering groceries online

Sunday
Preparing ingredients / cooking meals

CHAPTER 1

EXPRESS DINNERS

These recipes are for nights when you're not sure what to have, but you want it FAST. They are all about maximum flavour in minimum time – we're talking 20 minutes cooking for most of them.

I created this chapter because I know what it's like to be juggling a million things and still want to eat something nourishing (and not just toast for dinner… again). These are the go-to meals that save me during the week.

Beef burger bowls

SERVES 4
PREP TIME 10 minutes
COOK TIME 20 minutes

These burger bowls are seriously so good! They are on rotation at my place every week as they are light yet super satisfying.

2 tablespoons olive oil
500 g (1 lb 2 oz) extra-lean beef mince
1 brown onion, finely diced
1 teaspoon onion powder
½ teaspoon dried oregano
½ teaspoon smoked paprika
1 teaspoon salt flakes
½ teaspoon white pepper

CRISPY POTATOES
4 large white potatoes, diced
3 tablespoons olive oil
½ teaspoon sweet paprika
½ teaspoon dried oregano
½ teaspoon garlic powder
Juice of ½ lemon

BURGER SAUCE (OPTIONAL)
½ cup (120 g) whole-egg mayo
2 gherkins, finely diced
2 sprigs dill, finely chopped
1 tablespoon tomato sauce
1 tablespoon yellow mustard
1 garlic clove, crushed

TOPPINGS
1 iceberg lettuce, chopped
1 tomato, diced
½ red onion, diced
¼ cup (40 g) sliced pickles

1. To make the crispy potatoes, combine the potatoes with the olive oil, paprika, oregano, garlic powder and lemon juice in a large bowl and toss until coated. Season with salt and freshly ground black pepper and toss to combine. Transfer to an air fryer and cook at 180°C (350°F) for 20 minutes, or bake in a fan-forced oven at the same temperature for 30 minutes, until golden and crispy.
2. Meanwhile, heat the olive oil in a large frying pan over medium heat. Cook the mince, breaking it up with a spoon, for 3 minutes or until lightly browned. Add the onion, onion powder, oregano, paprika, salt and white pepper. Continue cooking for 5–6 minutes or until the onion is softened and the mince is fully cooked through. Set aside.
3. To make the burger sauce, combine all the ingredients in a medium bowl. Season with salt. Mix until smooth.
4. We're ready to assemble! Divide the crispy potatoes, mince mixture, lettuce, tomato, red onion and pickles between serving bowls. Sprinkle with a little salt, then dollop with burger sauce to serve.

Leah's notes There is no harm in store-bought sauce! If you know you love a certain one, use that instead of making your own for a quicker, easier dinner.

Teriyaki salmon bowls

SERVES 4
PREP TIME 10 minutes
COOK TIME 10 minutes

The hero of this recipe is the homemade teriyaki sauce; it is so simple to make and uses ingredients easily found in the pantry.

4 × 200 g (7 oz) salmon fillets
1 tablespoon olive oil
2 cups (370 g) cooked brown rice
1 large avocado, thickly sliced
1 large carrot, julienned
1 cup (160 g) edamame beans, cooked according to packet instructions
1 small cucumber, cut into ribbons
2 spring onions (scallions), thinly sliced

TERIYAKI SAUCE
½ cup (125 ml) soy sauce
⅓ cup (80 ml) oyster sauce
2 tablespoons honey, warmed
2 tablespoons grated ginger
3–4 garlic cloves, grated
2 small red chillies, diced (optional)

1. To make the teriyaki sauce, mix together all the ingredients in a shallow dish. Set aside 4 tablespoons to use later.
2. Add the salmon fillets to the remaining teriyaki sauce, and turn to coat the fish.
3. Heat the oil in a frying pan over medium heat. Cook the salmon skin-side down for 2–3 minutes or until the skin is crisp. Once the skin is crisp, cook, turning occasionally, for 8 minutes or until cooked to your liking.
4. Divide the brown rice between the bowls and top with the avocado, carrot, edamame beans and cucumber. Place a salmon fillet on each bowl and drizzle with the reserved teriyaki sauce. Sprinkle with sliced spring onions to serve.

Leah's notes If you have extra time, the salmon can be marinated overnight or for a few hours. Keep the reserved teriyaki sauce in the fridge until you are ready to cook.

Swedish meatballs and pasta

SERVES 4
PREP TIME 10 minutes
COOK TIME 30 minutes

Gravy and meatballs? Name a more delicious combo. This recipe takes a little longer as you quick-fry the meatballs before baking, but it's a great one to make in bulk and freeze.

500 g (1 lb 2 oz) pork and veal mince
1 teaspoon salt
1 teaspoon pepper
¼ teaspoon ground allspice
¼ teaspoon freshly grated nutmeg
Pinch of white (granulated) sugar
Pinch of ground ginger
1 brown onion, finely diced
2 garlic cloves, crushed
¼ cup (60 ml) pure (single/pouring) cream
1 egg
¼ cup (30 g) fine breadcrumbs
1 tablespoon olive oil
½ cup (125 ml) chicken stock
500 g (1 lb 2 oz) penne pasta
Chopped flat-leaf parsley, to serve

GRAVY
¼ cup (60 g) butter
¼ cup (35 g) plain (all-purpose) flour
2 cups (500 ml) beef or chicken stock
½ cup (125 g) sour cream

Leah's notes You can use 250 g (9 oz) beef and 250 g (9 oz) pork mince instead.

1. Preheat the oven to 180°C (350°F) fan-forced.
2. Place the mince in a bowl and add the salt, pepper, allspice, nutmeg, sugar, ground ginger, onion and garlic. Pour in the cream, egg and breadcrumbs and stir until well combined.
3. Using about 1–2 tablespoons of mince mixture at a time, roll into meatballs, ensuring they are roughly the same size. Continue until all the mixture is used up.
4. Heat the oil in a large frying pan and cook the meatballs, turning often, until brown all over. The meatballs do not need to be fully cooked, just golden brown on the outside.
5. Transfer the meatballs to a large baking dish and carefully pour the chicken stock over them.
6. Bake for about 20 minutes or until the meatballs are completely cooked through.
7. Meanwhile, bring a large saucepan of salted water to the boil. Add the pasta and cook according to the packet instructions. Drain the pasta well, reserving ¼ cup (60 ml) of the water, and return to the pan.
8. Transfer the meatballs to a plate and keep the juices in the baking dish. Stir through a little extra stock or water and scrape the bottom to get all the flavour, then transfer to a large frying pan.
9. To make the gravy, add the butter to the frying pan and heat until simmering. Add the plain flour, stirring continuously. Slowly add in the pasta water and the stock and season to taste. Stir through the sour cream, mixing well until smooth and thickened.
10. Once the gravy is finished, add the meatballs and cook until warmed through. Divide pasta between bowls and top with meatballs and gravy. Sprinkle with parsley to serve.

Pesto pasta salad

SERVES 4–6
PREP TIME 15 minutes
COOK TIME 10 minutes

If you want a fresh pasta salad recipe – this is it. The zestiness of the lemon and homemade pesto makes this extra special. I love to eat this one hot or cold.

500 g (1 lb 2 oz) farfalle (bow-tie) pasta
350 g (12 oz) mixed cherry or grape tomatoes, halved
220 g (7¾ oz) bocconcini, drained and halved

PESTO
2 cups firmly packed (100 g) basil leaves
2 cups (90 g) baby spinach leaves
1 cup (100 g) grated parmesan
¼ cup (40 g) toasted pine nuts
2 small garlic cloves
150 ml (5 fl oz) lemon juice
250 ml (9 fl oz) extra virgin olive oil
1 teaspoon each salt and freshly ground black pepper

1. Bring a large saucepan of salted water to the boil. Add the pasta and cook according to the packet instructions. Drain well, rinse with cold water and transfer to a large bowl.
2. Meanwhile, place the basil, spinach, parmesan, pine nuts and garlic in a food processor. Blend for 10 seconds or until combined.
3. Add the lemon juice and, while blending, slowly drizzle in the olive oil to form a smooth runny paste.
4. Season with the salt and pepper.
5. Pour the pesto dressing into the cooked pasta. Add the tomatoes and bocconcini and fold everything together.
6. Divide into bowls or containers.

Leah's notes The addition of baby spinach in this pesto gives the salad a beautiful vibrant green colour. This makes a great side dish or is equally substantial as a complete meal. It's also perfect to divide into containers for a grab-and-go lunch during the working week.

Beef and cashew stir-fry

SERVES 4
PREP TIME 10 minutes
COOK TIME 10 minutes

This one is inspired by my favourite Thai dish and I love the nuttiness of the roasted cashews. We love this served with steamed rice to soak up all the sauce.

¼ cup (60 ml) light soy sauce
¼ cup (60 ml) oyster sauce
1 tablespoon rice vinegar
2 tablespoons brown sugar
2 garlic cloves, crushed
1 teaspoon grated ginger
1 teaspoon dry chilli flakes
1 tablespoon cornflour (cornstarch)
¼ cup (60 ml) water
1 tablespoon sesame oil
500 g (1 lb 2 oz) lean beef mince
4 cups fresh vegetables of your choice, chopped
1 cup (155 g) roasted cashews
½ bunch spring onions (scallions), thinly sliced
2 tablespoons toasted sesame seeds, to garnish
Steamed rice, to serve

1. In a small bowl, mix together the soy sauce, oyster sauce, vinegar, brown sugar, garlic, ginger, chilli flakes, cornflour and water until smooth and combined.
2. Heat the sesame oil in a large pan or wok over high heat. Stir-fry the beef, breaking it up with a spoon, for 5 minutes or until evenly cooked.
3. Add the vegetables and sauce and stir-fry for 2–3 minutes or until the sauce has thickened and the vegetables are just tender.
4. Remove from the heat and add the cashews and spring onion. Gently fold to combine.
5. Top with sesame seeds and serve with steamed rice.

Leah's notes You can use whatever fresh vegetables you have available in your fridge, or pre-packaged fresh or frozen stir-fry mixes work equally well. This is delicious with steamed rice, noodles or just on its own.

Steak and peppercorn sauce with mash

SERVES 4
PREP TIME 10 minutes
COOK TIME 20 minutes

This is a great way to mix up the usual steak dinner. The peppercorn sauce is such a good combo with the steak, plus the mash to soak it all up – winner for sure! Definitely give this one a go.

4 large white potatoes, peeled and diced
500 g (1 lb 2 oz) green beans, trimmed and halved
4 × 200 g (7 oz) porterhouse steaks, trimmed
Olive oil, for coating steak
2–3 tablespoons steak seasoning (or paprika, onion powder, garlic powder)
3 tablespoons (60 g) butter
1 teaspoon garlic salt

PEPPERCORN SAUCE
1 tablespoon (20 g) butter
½ teaspoon freshly ground black pepper
1 small shallot, finely diced
2 tablespoons tinned green peppercorns plus 1 tablespoon peppercorn brine
½ cup (125 ml) beef stock
2 teaspoons dijon mustard
½ teaspoon Worcestershire sauce
250 ml (9 fl oz) thickened (heavy/pouring) cream

1. In a large pot of boiling water, cook the potatoes for about 15 minutes, or until they're tender and easily pierced with a fork. In the final 2 minutes of cooking, add the green beans to the pot to lightly cook. Drain and set both aside.
2. Meanwhile, make the peppercorn sauce. Melt the butter in a small saucepan over medium heat. Add the black pepper, shallot, green peppercorns and brine. Sauté for 3–5 minutes, or until the shallot is softened. Stir in the stock, dijon mustard, Worcestershire sauce and thickened cream. Mix well and simmer for about 15 minutes until reduced and thickened.
3. Rub the steaks with olive oil and season generously with steak seasoning. Grill on a barbecue or sear in a hot pan until cooked to your preferred doneness. *(Refer to Leah's notes for timing.)* Set steaks aside to rest for 5 minutes before slicing.
4. While the steaks are resting, mash the boiled potatoes with the butter and garlic salt to taste, until smooth and creamy.
5. Divide the mashed potato between plates and top with sliced steak and green beans. Generously spoon the peppercorn sauce over the meal. Serve immediately.

Leah's notes Cooking steak is a tricky one, but the easiest thing to remember is time! For a steak that's the thickness of a knuckle, cook for 2 minutes on each side for rare, 3 minutes on each side for medium, 4 minutes on each side for medium well and 5 minutes each side for well done.

Pesto chicken pita pizzas

SERVES 4
PREP TIME 10 minutes
COOK TIME 15 minutes

Pita pizzas are a staple in this house! The pita bread makes the perfect pizza base with little effort – I love mixing up the topping to suit what leftovers we have in the fridge. This chicken and pesto style is definitely one of our favourites to make.

2 tablespoons olive oil, plus extra to drizzle
2 small boneless, skinless chicken breasts, diced
4 medium pita breads
190 g (6¾ oz) jar basil pesto
500 g (1 lb 2 oz) grated mozzarella cheese
½ red onion, thinly sliced
1 cup (220 g) marinated artichokes, cut into quarters
1 cup (45 g) baby rocket (arugula)
½ cup (50 g) shaved parmesan

1. Preheat the oven to 200°C (400°F) fan-forced.
2. Heat the olive oil in a large frying pan over high heat and cook the chicken for 5–6 minutes or until cooked through. Transfer to a plate using a slotted spoon.
3. Place pita breads on lined oven trays and evenly spread each bread with 2 tablespoons pesto.
4. Sprinkle half the grated mozzarella on each base, then add the cooked chicken, red onion and artichokes. Top with the remaining mozzarella.
5. Bake for 6–8 minutes or until the cheese is melted and golden brown. Keep an eye on them as they can burn easily.
6. Transfer pizzas to a board and cut into quarters.
7. Divide between plates and top with rocket, parmesan and a drizzle of olive oil.

Leah's notes If you are really short on time, a barbecue chicken from the shops will make this even quicker.

Meatball pita pockets

SERVES 4
PREP TIME 10 minutes
COOK TIME 15 minutes

We love meatballs in this house, so that usually means I have a freezer stash ready to go. Serving these ones in pita pockets keeps everything together, and the salad brings so much freshness.

1 tablespoon olive oil
400 g (14 oz) beef meatballs
200 g (7 oz) haloumi
4 pita pockets
2 cups (80 g) salad leaves
2 large vine-ripened tomatoes, sliced
2 Lebanese (short) cucumbers, sliced
½ red onion, thinly sliced
400 g (14 oz) tzatziki

1. Heat the oil in a frying pan over medium heat. Cook the meatballs, turning frequently, for 10–12 minutes or until cooked through. Set aside and cover to keep warm.
2. Slice the haloumi into eight even slices. Heat a non-stick frying pan over medium heat and cook the haloumi for 2–3 minutes each side or until golden.
3. Heat the pita pockets in the microwave according to the packet instructions.
4. Cut the pita pockets open and begin layering in the salad leaves, tomato, cucumber, red onion, haloumi and meatballs.
5. Finish with a generous dollop of tzatziki to serve.

Leah's notes If you would like to mix it up from beef meatballs, some lamb or pork would be delicious in this recipe too – use whatever is your favourite.

Buffalo chicken sliders

SERVES 4

PREP TIME 10 minutes

COOK TIME 10 minutes

Buffalo chicken and sliders are a match made in heaven. The buns are perfect to soak up all the juices of the chicken. I love to use aioli or ranch, but use whatever sauce you love the most.

2 large boneless, skinless chicken breasts, cut in half lengthways
3 tablespoons (60 g) butter
4–8 slider bread rolls, halved
100 ml (3½ fl oz) aioli or ranch dressing
1 small head cos lettuce

BUFFALO SPICE MIX

2 tablespoons brown sugar
1 tablespoon garlic powder
1 tablespoon onion powder
1 tablespoon smoked paprika
¼ teaspoon chilli powder
¼ teaspoon cayenne pepper (optional)
1 teaspoon salt
1 teaspoon freshly ground black pepper

1. To make the Buffalo spice mix, combine all the ingredients in a large bowl. Mix thoroughly.
2. Coat the chicken breasts in the Buffalo spice mix, rubbing it in all over.
3. Melt the butter in a large non-stick frying pan over medium heat. Cook the chicken for 5 minutes each side or until cooked through. Transfer to a bowl and use two forks to shred the chicken while still hot.
4. Lightly toast the bread rolls and spread each base with aioli or ranch dressing.
5. Divide the rolls between plates and top with torn lettuce leaves. Spoon a generous amount of cooked chicken on each. Finish with the tops of the rolls and serve.

Leah's notes This recipe can easily be doubled or tripled for a crowd. The chicken can even be cooked, shredded then frozen for a fast meal. Thaw and reheat in a frying pan with a little oil.

Creamy prawn and tomato pasta

SERVES 4
PREP TIME 10 minutes
COOK TIME 20 minutes

Who doesn't love a delicious prawn pasta? This recipe is such a good one to make for a lot of people as it can easily be doubled. I sometimes use vegetable stock instead of chicken and it works just as well. Add extra chilli flakes if you love it spicy!

500 g (1 lb 2 oz) linguine pasta
2 tablespoons olive oil
2 tablespoons (40 g) butter
800 g (1 lb 12 oz) raw prawns, peeled and deveined
2 garlic cloves, finely chopped
1 teaspoon dried chilli flakes
1 brown onion, thinly sliced
150 ml (5 fl oz) white wine
1 cup (210 g) semi-dried tomatoes, drained and blended to a paste
2 tablespoons tomato paste (concentrated purée)
200 ml (7 fl oz) light cooking cream
200 ml (7 fl oz) chicken stock
1 handful flat-leaf parsley, chopped

1. Bring a large pot of salted water to the boil and cook the pasta according to the packet instructions. Drain and set aside.
2. While the pasta is cooking, heat the olive oil and butter in a large, deep frying pan over medium heat.
3. Cook the prawns, garlic, and chilli flakes for 2–3 minutes or until the prawns are just cooked through. Remove the prawns from the pan and set aside.
4. Add the onion to the frying pan and cook for 3–4 minutes or until softened. Pour in the white wine and simmer for 2 minutes or until slightly reduced.
5. Stir in the semi-dried tomato paste, tomato paste, light cooking cream and chicken stock. Mix gently to combine and reduce the heat to low. Cook for 5–8 minutes or until the sauce is thickened.
6. Return the cooked prawns to the pan along with the pasta. Toss gently to coat and warm through.
7. Remove from the heat, fold in the chopped parsley and divide between bowls. Serve immediately.

Leah's notes The white wine is totally optional in this recipe, just leave it out if you prefer.

Prawn and pesto pine nut pasta

SERVES 4

PREP TIME 15 minutes

COOK TIME 10 minutes

I love using prawns in pasta to change up the protein. The pine nuts add a delicious nutty flavour to this recipe. Double or triple the pesto in this recipe as it freezes so well!

500 g (1 lb 2 oz) rigatoni pasta
1 tablespoon olive oil
500 g (1 lb 2 oz) raw prawns, peeled and deveined
2 × 90 g (3¼ oz) fresh burrata

BASIL AND SPINACH PESTO

2 cups firmly packed (100 g) basil leaves
2 cups (90 g) baby spinach leaves
1 cup (100 g) grated parmesan
¼ cup (40 g) toasted pine nuts (or sub with cashews/walnuts), plus extra to serve
2 small garlic cloves
150 ml (5 fl oz) lemon juice, plus wedges to serve
1 cup (250 ml) extra virgin olive oil
1 teaspoon each salt and freshly ground black pepper

1. To make the pesto, blitz the basil, spinach, parmesan, pine nuts and garlic in a food processor for 10 seconds. Add the lemon juice and, while blending, slowly drizzle in the extra virgin olive oil to form a smooth, runny paste. Add the salt and pepper and blitz to combine.
2. Bring a large pot of salted water to the boil and cook the rigatoni according to the packet instructions. Drain and return to the pot.
3. Pour the pesto over the hot pasta and toss to combine.
4. Heat the olive oil in a medium frying pan over high heat. Sear the prawns for 1 minute each side or until just cooked through. Add the cooked prawns to the pasta. Gently mix to combine.
5. Transfer to a serving bowl. Top with the burrata and sprinkle with extra pine nuts. Serve with lemon wedges.

Leah's notes Any pasta would work with this recipe, just use what you have on hand if you can't find rigatoni.

Lemon chipotle salmon with salsa

SERVES 4
PREP TIME 15 minutes
COOK TIME 6 minutes

I love the flavours in chipotle seasoning. One day I decided to sprinkle it over my salmon before cooking – let me tell you, it was a game changer! This with the zinginess of the lemon creates so much flavour and is a great way to spice up your salmon.

4 medium tomatoes, diced
2 Lebanese (short) cucumbers, diced
½ red onion, finely diced
1 small handful coriander (cilantro), roughly chopped, plus leaves to garnish
2 tablespoons sliced pickled jalapeños, finely diced
⅓ cup (80 ml) extra virgin olive oil
Juice of 2 lemons plus wedges to serve
1 teaspoon each salt and freshly ground black pepper
¼ cup (35 g) chipotle seasoning
4 salmon fillets
2 tablespoons olive oil

1. In a medium bowl, combine the tomato, cucumber, red onion, chopped coriander, jalapeño, extra virgin olive oil and the juice of 1 lemon. Season with salt and pepper.
2. Sprinkle the chipotle seasoning evenly over the salmon.
3. Heat the olive oil in a large non-stick frying pan over high heat. Sear the salmon for 3 minutes each side or until golden and cooked to your liking. Add the remaining lemon juice to the pan.
4. Divide the salmon between plates and top with the salsa. Garnish with coriander leaves and serve with lemon wedges.

Leah's notes Chipotle can add some kick – use a little less if you aren't a big fan of spice.

Bruschetta chicken

SERVES 2
PREP TIME 10 minutes
COOK TIME 5 minutes

This one is a more simple recipe, ready for you to jazz up if you have the time! You can add a carbohydrate here to bulk out the meal or keep it lighter, up to you. I would add some roast potatoes if I wanted a little extra – yum!

1 large boneless, skinless chicken breast
1 large ripe tomato, diced
10 basil leaves, chopped, plus extra leaves to serve
½ red onion, thinly sliced
1 garlic clove, crushed
2 tablespoons olive oil, plus extra to drizzle
2 tablespoons basil pesto
Balsamic glaze, to drizzle

1. Slice the chicken breast horizontally into thin schnitzels, you should get at least four out of a chicken breast. Season with salt and freshly ground black pepper.
2. Combine the tomato, basil, red onion, garlic and a drizzle of olive oil in a small bowl. Season with salt and pepper. Mix well to combine.
3. Heat the olive oil in a large frying pan over medium heat. Cook the chicken for 1–2 minutes each side or until lightly golden and cooked through. Transfer to plates.
4. Smear pesto across each piece of chicken and top with the tomato mixture.
5. Drizzle with balsamic glaze and serve with extra basil leaves.

Leah's notes If you want to make this vegetarian, swap the chicken for haloumi – it works just as well and tastes amazing too.

Beef noodle soup

SERVES 2
PREP TIME 10 minutes
COOK TIME 20 minutes

This is a perfect one for a winter's day, or if you're feeling unwell – it's so hearty without the huge effort!

2 tablespoons olive oil
2 cm (¾ in) piece of ginger, grated
1 garlic clove, crushed
1 red chilli, finely chopped, plus extra, sliced, to serve
3 cups (750 ml) beef stock
½ cup (125 ml) water
2 teaspoons soy sauce
Juice of ½ lime
1 small carrot, cut into matchsticks
1 spring onion (scallion), thinly sliced
1 bok choy, leaves separated
3 broccolini stalks, roughly chopped
200 g (9 oz) dried rice noodles
200 g (7 oz) rump steak, sliced extra thinly
1 handful bean sprouts
1 handful coriander (cilantro)
Chilli sauce, to drizzle (optional)

1. Heat the olive oil in a large pot over medium heat. Cook the ginger, garlic and chilli for about 3 minutes or until softened and fragrant.
2. Pour in the beef stock, water, soy sauce and lime juice. Stir and bring to a gentle simmer.
3. Add the carrot, spring onion, bok choy and broccolini. Simmer for 5–6 minutes or until the vegetables are just tender.
4. Add the noodles and thinly sliced steak to the pot. Cook for 3–5 minutes or until the noodles are soft and the steak is just cooked through. Slicing the steak thinly means it cooks quickly in the broth.
5. Divide the noodles, vegetables and steak between serving bowls. Ladle the hot broth over the top.
6. Top each bowl with bean sprouts, coriander and sliced chilli. For extra heat, drizzle with chilli sauce to taste.

Leah's notes If you're struggling to thinly slice the beef, place it in the freezer for 20 minutes and it will become easier.

Veggie and chicken noodle stir-fry

SERVES 4
PREP TIME 15 minutes
COOK TIME 20 minutes

Stir-fries are the ultimate meal prep – this reheats so well as the noodles soak up all the flavours. I love the aromas that the fresh ginger and garlic add to this recipe.

300 g (10½ oz) fresh egg noodles
1 tablespoon olive oil
300 g (10½ oz) chicken tenderloins
½ brown onion, thinly sliced
3–4 garlic cloves, crushed
1 tablespoon grated ginger
1 red chilli, sliced (optional)
4 button mushrooms, sliced
¼ white cabbage, shredded
1 carrot, julienned
½ small head broccoli, cut into bite-sized pieces
½ red capsicum (pepper), thinly sliced
Thinly sliced red chilli and fried shallots, to garnish

STIR-FRY SAUCE
2 tablespoons soy sauce
1 tablespoon dark soy sauce
2 tablespoons oyster sauce
1 teaspoon gochujang (Korean chilli paste)
¼ cup (60 ml) water
1 tablespoon cornflour (cornstarch)

1. Cook the egg noodles according to the packet directions. Drain and set aside.
2. To make the stir-fry sauce, combine all the ingredients in a small bowl. Mix well until smooth and set aside.
3. Heat the olive oil in a large frying pan over medium heat. Cook the chicken for 5–6 minutes each side or until lightly browned. Transfer to a plate. Cook the onion for 2–3 minutes or until lightly translucent.
4. Add the garlic, ginger and chilli (if using). Stir-fry for 1 minute or until fragrant.
5. Add the sliced mushrooms, cabbage, carrot and broccoli and stir-fry for 2–3 minutes or until lightly softened.
6. Add the capsicum and stir-fry for another minute or until just tender. Return the chicken to the pan.
7. Add the noodles and use tongs to toss and combine. Add the stir-fry sauce and give it a good mix to coat everything.
8. Sprinkle with chilli and fried shallots before serving.

Leah's notes If you want to make this even quicker, use frozen veg!

CHAPTER 2

ONE-POT MAIN MEALS

These are my go-tos for those nights when life is hectic and you just need something easy, quick and delicious on the table, without making a massive mess in the kitchen. As a busy mum, time is so valuable – that's why I LOVE a good one-pot meal (though sometimes I use an extra pot to boil up some pasta). It's the kind of cooking that works with your life, not against it.

These recipes are perfect for when you've had a huge day, the kids are running around and you just need dinner to sort itself out while you catch your breath. They're simple, delicious and full of flavour and, best of all, they'll save your sanity midweek!

Vodka pasta with chicken and spinach

SERVES 4
PREP TIME 10 minutes
COOK TIME 30 minutes

This recipe is so good to make when feeding a lot of people, because it's simple enough to make for a crowd but also the quickest dinner!

1 tablespoon (20 g) butter
2 French shallots, finely diced
4 garlic cloves, crushed
¼ cup (60 g) tomato paste (concentrated purée)
½ teaspoon chilli flakes
1 shot (30 ml) vodka (optional)
400 g (14 oz) tin crushed tomatoes
330 ml (11¼ fl oz) thickened (heavy/whipping) cream
200 g (7 oz) boneless, skinless chicken breast, cut into bite-sized pieces
2 handfuls baby spinach
400 g (14 oz) rigatoni pasta
Grated parmesan cheese, to serve

1. Melt the butter in a large frying pan over medium heat. Add the shallots and garlic and cook for 2–3 minutes or until translucent and fragrant.
2. Stir in the tomato paste and cook for 1-2 minutes or until darkened in colour. Add the chilli flakes and season with salt and freshly ground black pepper. Now, add your vodka (if using) and allow the alcohol to cook out, this will only take a minute.
3. Add the tomatoes, thickened cream and chicken breast and cook for 20 minutes.
4. Stir in the spinach and cook for 2 minutes or until wilted.
5. Meanwhile, bring a large saucepan of salted water to the boil. Cook the pasta for 1-2 minutes less than specified on the packet instructions.
6. Drain the pasta, saving some of the pasta water.
7. Add the pasta to the sauce along with a splash of pasta water and stir through gently to combine. Cook for a minute or so until the pasta is al dente.
8. Serve immediately, topped with parmesan.

Leah's notes Vodka is optional in this recipe – I use it if we're given a bottle, but if you're not a vodka drinker, skip it or just purchase one of the little bottles!

Chicken fajita rice

SERVES 4

PREP TIME 10 minutes

COOK TIME 20 minutes

This is a great dish to make ahead of time as it reheats well – perfect for lunch the next day!

400 g (14 oz) boneless, skinless chicken breast, thinly sliced
1 tablespoon olive oil, plus extra to drizzle
2 green, yellow or red capsicums (peppers), thinly sliced
2 garlic cloves, crushed
1 red onion, finely diced
1 cup (200 g) basmati rice, rinsed
¼ cup (50 g) tinned black beans, drained and rinsed
2 cups (500 ml) chicken stock
Lime wedges, to serve

FAJITA SPICE MIX

1 teaspoon smoked paprika
½ teaspoon chilli powder
1 teaspoon ground cumin
1 teaspoon onion powder
1 teaspoon dried oregano

1. To make the fajita spice mix, combine all the ingredients in a small bowl. Season with salt and freshly ground black pepper.
2. Combine the chicken breast and half the spice mix in a large bowl. Drizzle with olive oil and gently toss until the chicken is completely coated.
3. Heat the olive oil in a large deep saucepan over medium heat. Cook the chicken strips, stirring, for 5 minutes or until half cooked, then add the capsicum, garlic and onion.
4. Cook for 3–4 minutes or until the vegetables are beginning to soften.
5. Add the rice, the remaining spice mix and the black beans and stir until well combined.
6. Add the chicken stock and a pinch of salt and pepper and cover with a lid. Turn down to a simmer and cook for 13 minutes or until the rice is cooked through.
7. To serve, add a generous squeeze of fresh lime juice.

Leah's notes You can use less chilli powder if your family isn't a fan. For a creamier finish, stir a little sour cream into the rice.

Philly cheesesteak buns

SERVES 4
PREP TIME 10 minutes
COOK TIME 10 minutes

The perfect 'fakeaway' dinner on a Friday night, we love this as a quick meal after a long week!

2 tablespoons olive oil
1 small brown onion, thinly sliced
2 garlic cloves, crushed
1 green capsicum (pepper), diced
½ teaspoon smoked paprika
½ teaspoon chilli powder
500 g (1 lb 2 oz) beef rump steak, thinly sliced (the thinner the better)
4 long bread rolls
⅓ cup (85 g) aioli
4 slices provolone cheese

1. Heat the olive oil in a large frying pan over medium heat. When the oil is hot, cook the onion, garlic and capsicum for 2–3 minutes or until the onion is translucent.
2. Stir in the paprika and chilli powder and cook for 1 minute or until fragrant. Be careful not to burn the spices. Season with salt and freshly ground black pepper.
3. Add the sliced steak to the pan and cook, stirring, for 5 minutes or until fully cooked through.
4. Meanwhile, slice the rolls in half and lightly toast until golden. Generously spread with the garlic aioli.
5. Divide the steak mixture between the four prepared rolls. Immediately top with cheese so it melts and serve.

Leah's notes If you don't have steak on hand, chicken breast can work well here too.

Chicken and lemon risoni

SERVES 4

PREP TIME 10 minutes

COOK TIME 20 minutes

We love a one-pot meal when we don't want a massive clean-up! Lemony dinners are so fresh, and this one is especially good in the summer when your time is better spent outside.

2 tablespoons olive oil
1 brown onion, finely diced
1 teaspoon thyme, finely chopped
300 g (10½ oz) boneless, skinless chicken breast, thinly sliced
3 garlic cloves, crushed
Grated zest and juice of 1 lemon
3 cups (750 ml) vegetable stock
⅔ cup (125 g) risoni (orzo)
2 big handfuls baby spinach
100 g (3½ oz) feta cheese, crumbled

1. Heat the olive oil in a deep pan over medium heat. Add the onion and thyme and season with salt and freshly ground black pepper. Cook for 2–3 minutes or until the onion is translucent.
2. Add the sliced chicken breast and cook, stirring, for 1-2 minutes or until browned.
3. Add the garlic and lemon zest to the pan and cook for 1–2 minutes. Add the vegetable stock, lemon juice and risoni and reduce the heat to low. Cook, stirring occasionally, for 8 minutes or until the risoni is almost al dente, and then add the spinach. Season with salt and pepper and cook until the chicken and risoni are completely cooked through.
4. Remove from the heat and serve topped with crumbled feta.

Leah's notes Use chicken stock if you don't have any vegetable stock.

Thai basil chicken

SERVES 4
PREP TIME 10 minutes
COOK TIME 20 minutes

This recipe packs in so much flavour! We love serving it with rice to soak up all the delicious juices.

2 tablespoons sesame oil
1 brown onion, finely diced
1 long red chilli, deseeded and finely chopped
1 tablespoon grated ginger
3 garlic cloves, crushed
4 button mushrooms, finely diced
1 zucchini (courgette), grated
500 g (1 lb 2 oz) chicken mince
¼ teaspoon fennel seeds
¼ teaspoon cayenne pepper
½ teaspoon salt
½ teaspoon freshly ground black pepper
100 g (3½ oz) string beans, trimmed and halved
1 small red capsicum (pepper), thinly sliced
10 Thai basil leaves
2 tablespoons soy sauce
1 tablespoon oyster sauce
Steamed rice, to serve

1. Heat the sesame oil in a wok over medium heat.
2. Once the oil is hot, cook the onion, chilli, ginger and garlic for 2–3 minutes or until the onion is translucent.
3. Add the mushroom and zucchini and stir-fry for 3–4 minutes or until lightly browned.
4. Add the chicken mince and break it up into smaller pieces. Add the fennel seeds, cayenne pepper, salt and black pepper to the mixture and stir-fry for 6–8 minutes or until the chicken is almost cooked through.
5. Add the beans, capsicum and Thai basil and stir-fry for 3 minutes or until softened.
6. Stir in the soy sauce and oyster sauce and cook for 1 minute or until combined. Serve on steamed rice.

Leah's notes You can swap in any veggies you have on hand for this recipe, it is perfect for using up ingredients so they don't go to waste.

Eggplant arrabiata

SERVES 4
PREP TIME 10 minutes
COOK TIME 30 minutes

This is our go-to vegetarian meal, perfect as a side dish or main. Eggplant is one of those vegetables that's so great for soaking up all the flavour.

⅓ cup (80 ml) olive oil
2 eggplants (aubergines), cut into cubes
1 brown onion, finely diced
1 long red chilli, finely chopped
3–4 garlic cloves, crushed
2 tablespoons flat-leaf parsley, finely chopped
2 × 400 g (14 oz) tins crushed tomatoes
1 teaspoon white (granulated) sugar
10 Sicilian olives, pitted and halved
400 g (14 oz) penne (or short pasta of your choice)
Grated parmesan cheese, to serve

1. Heat the olive oil in a deep pan over medium heat. Add half the eggplant with a big pinch of salt and cook, stirring occasionally, for 7–8 minutes or until the eggplant is golden brown and slightly softened. Repeat with the remaining eggplant, then return it all to the pan.
2. Add the onion and chilli and cook for 2–3 minutes, then stir in the garlic to ensure it doesn't burn. Add half the parsley and season with freshly ground black pepper. Cook for 1 minute to heat through.
3. Add the tomatoes, sugar and olives and cook for a further 15 minutes or until the eggplant is fully softened.
4. Meanwhile, bring a large saucepan of salted water to the boil. Cook the penne until almost al dente, then drain and add the penne to the sauce to soak up that flavour as it finishes cooking.
5. Serve topped with parmesan cheese and the remaining parsley.

Leah's notes The fresh chilli can be swapped for chilli flakes or left out completely if you aren't a fan of spice.

Baked veggie and feta pasta

SERVES 4

PREP TIME 10 minutes

COOK TIME 1 hour

The combination of feta and cherry tomatoes is such a winner here, it adds so much flavour and creaminess to the dish – we love this one.

400 g (14 oz) block feta cheese
400 g (14 oz) cherry tomatoes
Olive oil, for drizzling
2–3 garlic cloves, crushed
Dried oregano, for sprinkling
250 g (9 oz) pumpkin (squash), cut into cubes
1 red onion, cut into cubes
1 small zucchini (courgette), cut into cubes
1 red capsicum (pepper), cut into cubes
1 eggplant (aubergine), cut into cubes
300 g (10½ oz) fettuccine (or long pasta of your choice)

1. Preheat the oven to 180°C (350°F) fan-forced.
2. Place the block of feta in a baking dish (you can leave it whole) and cover with the cherry tomatoes. Drizzle the olive oil all over so they're covered well. Add the crushed garlic, sprinkle with dried oregano and season with salt and freshly ground black pepper. Bake for 40 minutes or until the tomatoes have burst and the feta is lightly browned.
3. On a separate lined baking tray, add the pumpkin, onion, zucchini, capsicum and eggplant. Drizzle generously with olive oil and sprinkle with dried oregano. Season with salt and pepper. Toss to completely coat. Bake for 30-40 minutes or until the veggies are tender.
4. Meanwhile, bring a large saucepan of salted water to the boil. Cook the pasta until al dente. Drain and set aside.
5. When the feta is ready, use a spoon to mix the feta and tomatoes together (it should be super soft!) then add the pasta. Mix through well, then add the vegetables and toss until all combined.

Leah's notes Chicken goes well with this dish if you are wanting to add a meat-based protein.

Taco rice bowls

SERVES 4
PREP TIME 10 minutes
COOK TIME 30 minutes

Taco Tuesdays just got a whole lot easier with this one-pot meal – the mix is perfect to eat on its own or added to a wrap to make a burrito. Yum!

500 g (1 lb 2 oz) beef mince
1 small brown onion, diced
3 garlic cloves, crushed
1 large red capsicum (pepper), diced
⅓ cup (35 g) taco seasoning
1 cup (250 g) tomato salsa
1 cup (200 g) basmati rice
400 g (14 oz) tin black beans, drained and rinsed
2½ cups (625 ml) beef stock
1 avocado, sliced
⅓ cup (85 g) sour cream
Chopped coriander (cilantro), grated Mexican cheese and salted corn chips, to serve

1. Cook the beef mince in a large frying pan over medium-high heat until lightly browned. There's no need to add any oil here, as the beef contains enough.
2. Add the onion, garlic and capsicum. Cook, stirring occasionally, until the vegetables are softened and the mince is cooked through.
3. Add the taco seasoning and tomato salsa and stir to coat and combine. Season with salt and freshly ground black pepper to taste.
4. Add the basmati rice, black beans and beef stock. Stir until well combined and reduce the heat to low. Cook, covered with a lid for 15 minutes or until the rice is tender.
5. Sprinkle with coriander. Serve with avocado, sour cream and cheese. Use the corn chips to scoop up the delicious mixture and eat!

Leah's notes If you don't have sour cream, plain Greek yoghurt works well too.

Saucy chilli con carne

SERVES 4

PREP TIME 10 minutes

COOK TIME 35 minutes

We love this meal on a cold winter's night – the spices make it so warming and comforting. Delicious!

2 tablespoons olive oil
1 small brown onion, diced
3 garlic cloves, crushed
1 red chilli, finely diced
1 red capsicum (pepper), diced
500 g (1 lb 2 oz) beef mince
400 g (14 oz) tin black beans, drained and rinsed
¼ cup (75 g) tomato paste (concentrated purée)
2 × 400 g (14 oz) tins crushed tomatoes
2 teaspoons curry powder
2 teaspoons mustard powder
1 teaspoon paprika
1 teaspoon ground cumin

SERVING SUGGESTIONS

Steamed basmati rice
1–2 tablespoons guacamole
1–2 tablespoons sour cream
Lime wedges, to serve

1. Heat the olive oil in a deep saucepan over medium–high heat. Add the onion, garlic, chilli and capsicum. Cook, stirring, for about 3 minutes or until the vegetables have softened. Ensure you are constantly stirring so the mixture doesn't burn.
2. Add the beef mince. Using a wooden spoon, break the mince into small pieces. Cook, stirring frequently, for 3-5 minutes or until the excess liquid has completely evaporated.
3. Add the black beans and tomato paste and cook, stirring, for 1 minute or until combined.
4. Add the tomatoes along with the curry powder, mustard powder, paprika and ground cumin. Mix well and simmer for 15 minutes. Taste and season to your liking with salt and freshly ground black pepper.
5. Reduce the heat to low and simmer for a further 10 minutes.
6. Serve the chilli over steamed rice with a dollop of guac, sour cream and a big squeeze of fresh lime.

Leah's notes If you don't have beef mince, pork or chicken mince work well here too.

Teriyaki salmon noodle stir-fry

SERVES 4
PREP TIME 10 minutes
COOK TIME 15 minutes

This is our favourite way to have salmon – the honey creates a delicious sticky glaze that coats the noodles perfectly. Toasting the sesame seeds really elevates this dish. Yum!

Olive oil, for cooking
2 salmon fillets, skin off
1 large carrot, thinly sliced
5 broccolini spears, roughly chopped
1 red capsicum (pepper), thinly sliced
500 g (1 lb 2 oz) thin fresh egg noodles, prepared according to packet directions
2 spring onions (scallions), thinly sliced
2 teaspoons toasted sesame seeds

JAPANESE-STYLE DRESSING

2 tablespoons soy sauce
2 tablespoons oyster sauce
1 tablespoon honey
1 teaspoon chilli oil
Juice of ½ lime
3 garlic cloves, crushed
1 cm (½ in) knob of ginger, grated

1. In a small bowl, make the Japanese-style dressing by combining all the ingredients.
2. In a medium frying pan, heat the olive oil over medium heat.
3. Add the salmon to the pan along with the carrot, broccolini and capsicum. Cook for around 12 minutes, flipping the salmon halfway and stirring the vegetables as needed.
4. When the salmon and vegetables are cooked through, break up the salmon in the pan. Give everything a really good mix to combine. Add the egg noodles and pour the dressing over the top. Reduce the heat to low and toss to combine.
5. Serve sprinkled with the spring onion and toasted sesame seeds.

Leah's notes You can swap in any veggies you have on hand, making it another great one for using up what's in your fridge.

Zingy chicken noodle soup

SERVES 4
PREP TIME 15 minutes
COOK TIME 25 minutes

The perfect winter soup to make when you are feeling a little run-down.

1 leek, thinly sliced
1 carrot, thinly sliced
2 stalks celery, finely chopped
3 garlic cloves, crushed
2 tablespoons thyme, finely chopped
1 tablespoon dried oregano
1 teaspoon smoked paprika
1 teaspoon ground turmeric
1 bay leaf
½ teaspoon chilli flakes (optional)
8 cups (2 litres) chicken stock
1 cup (150 g) shredded barbecue chicken
½ cup (125 ml) thickened (heavy/whipping) cream
Juice of 2 lemons
150 g (5½ oz) rice vermicelli noodles
Warm crusty bread, to serve

1. In a large saucepan over medium heat, add the leek, carrot, celery, garlic, thyme, oregano, paprika and turmeric. Season with salt and freshly ground black pepper. Cook, stirring, until the vegetables are lightly softened.
2. Add the bay leaf and chilli flakes (if using) and stir to combine. Add the chicken stock, shredded chicken, cream and juice of one lemon. Bring to a simmer, reduce the heat to low and cook for 15 minutes or until the veggies are tender.
3. Meanwhile, prepare the noodles according to the packet instructions.
4. Taste the broth, and season with more lemon juice, salt and pepper to your liking.
5. Divide the noodles between four bowls and ladle the broth over the top. Serve with warm, crusty bread.

Leah's notes Add the lemon juice slowly, tasting along the way to achieve your desired 'zinginess'.

Prawn laksa

SERVES 4
PREP TIME 10 minutes
COOK TIME 30 minutes

Who doesn't love a takeaway laksa? I used to go to a place in my hometown in Adelaide, it was a part of a food court but let me tell you... it was a secret GEM! This kickstarted my absolute love for laksa.

1 teaspoon olive oil
1 spring onion (scallion), sliced into large pieces
⅓ cup (90 g) laksa paste
2 × 400 ml (14 fl oz) tins coconut milk
2 cups (500 ml) vegetable stock
2 tablespoons soy sauce
2 tablespoons fish sauce, plus extra to serve
Juice of 1 large lime
2 baby bok choy, halved
20 banana prawns, peeled and deveined, tails on
500 g (1 lb 2 oz) thin egg noodles
1 small handful bean sprouts
Coriander (cilantro), to serve

1. Heat the olive oil in a deep saucepan over medium heat.
2. Cook the spring onion and laksa paste for 2 minutes or until fragrant and darkened. The deeper the colour goes, the more flavour comes out.
3. Add the coconut milk and vegetable stock and bring to a light simmer. Add soy sauce, fish sauce and lime juice. Taste here and season with salt and freshly ground black pepper to your liking.
4. Reduce the heat to low and simmer for 10 minutes. Add the bok choy and cook for 5 minutes or until almost tender. Add the prawns and cook for a further 5 minutes or until the prawns are cooked through.
5. Meanwhile, prepare the noodles according to the packet instructions.
6. Divide the noodles between four bowls. Top with the laksa soup, prawns and bok choy. Add a little extra fish sauce to taste. Sprinkle with bean sprouts and coriander to serve.

Leah's notes Prawns can be swapped for any other protein of your choice (salmon, chicken, dumplings, they all work perfectly!).

Green chicken curry

SERVES 4

PREP TIME 10 minutes

COOK TIME 30 minutes

This recipe is a Mama Itsines recipe, she used to make this for us for dinner after school and it was always a hit. Childhood memories unlocked!

2 tablespoons olive oil
2 boneless, skinless chicken breasts, cut into cubes
1 tablespoon vegetable oil
¼ cup (55 g) green curry paste (see below for a DIY version)
400 ml (14 fl oz) tin coconut cream
1 cup (250 ml) chicken stock
4 makrut lime leaves
2–3 cups of fresh veggies (such as mushroom, baby corn, snow peas or broccoli)
2–3 tablespoons fish sauce
Juice of 1 lime
1 handful Thai basil leaves
Steamed basmati rice, to serve

1. Heat the olive oil in a large deep saucepan over medium heat. Brown the chicken pieces in batches, seasoning each batch with salt and freshly ground black pepper. Transfer the cooked chicken to a plate and wipe out the pan.
2. Heat the vegetable oil in the saucepan over medium heat. Cook the curry paste, stirring, for 2–3 minutes or until fragrant.
3. Stir in the coconut cream, chicken stock and lime leaves and simmer for 5 minutes. Add the chicken and simmer for 15 minutes.
4. Add the vegetables to the curry and cook for a few minutes or until they soften to your liking.
5. Add the fish sauce, lime juice and Thai basil leaves.
6. Remove the lime leaves. Serve on steamed rice.

MAKE YOUR OWN CURRY PASTE IF YOU HAVE TIME!

2 teaspoons ground coriander
1 teaspoon ground black peppercorns
3–5 green chillies, seeded and finely chopped
1 tablespoon galangal powder or ground ginger
1 small handful coriander (cilantro) leaves, roughly chopped
2 large garlic cloves
2 spring onions (scallions)
1 lemongrass stalk, roughly chopped
2 tablespoons vegetable oil

Place the ingredients in a food processor and blend until the mixture forms a paste. Use as above, cooking for 3-4 minutes until fragrant before adding your liquid ingredients.

Leah's notes Chicken can be swapped for any other protein of your choice (I like this with tofu or salmon).

Eggplant and spicy chorizo pasta

SERVES 4
PREP TIME 10 minutes
COOK TIME 30 minutes

Eggplant is such an underrated vegetable to slide into sauces! It almost melts when cooked for long enough, so it's a really good one to use for bulk.

2 tablespoons olive oil
2 × 125 g (4½ oz) spicy chorizo sausages, sliced into half-moons
1 medium eggplant (aubergine), diced into bite-sized cubes
1 brown onion, finely diced
4 garlic cloves, crushed
¼ cup (55 g) semi-sundried tomatoes, diced
¼ cup (40 g) pitted kalamata olives, chopped
1 teaspoon dried oregano
5–8 basil leaves
1 cinnamon stick
800 g (1 lb 12 oz) tin chopped tomatoes
400 g (14 oz) penne pasta
2 cups (500 ml) chicken stock
Parmesan cheese, to serve

1. Heat the olive oil in a large saucepan over medium heat. Add the chorizo and cook until browned. Remove the chorizo from the pan and add a touch more olive oil. Add the eggplant and season with salt and freshly ground black pepper. Cook, stirring, for 5–7 minutes or until softened.
2. Add the onion and garlic and cook, stirring, until the onion is translucent.
3. Return the chorizo to the pan along with the semi-sundried tomatoes, olives, dried oregano, basil leaves, cinnamon and tinned tomatoes. Simmer for 5 minutes or until combined.
4. Add the uncooked pasta and the chicken stock. Reduce heat to low, cover with a lid and simmer for 10 minutes or until the pasta is al dente.
5. Grate parmesan into the mixture and stir through. Serve, topping with extra parmesan if you wish.

Leah's notes Swap chorizo for another mild sausage or a different protein altogether.

Coconut chicken rice

SERVES 4
PREP TIME 10 minutes
COOK TIME 25 minutes

Hearty but also light? YES! This recipe feels light and delicious but packs a punch with flavour, making it so perfect for any day of the week.

1 large lemongrass stalk, roughly chopped
2 French shallots, roughly chopped
3 cm (1¼ in) knob of ginger
4 makrut lime leaves
5 garlic cloves
1 tablespoon olive oil
1 tablespoon chilli crisp plus 1 tablespoon chilli oil
400 ml (14 fl oz) tin coconut milk
400 ml (14 fl oz) chicken stock
2 tablespoons fish sauce
2 tablespoons soy sauce
1 tablespoon brown sugar
6 boneless, skinless chicken thighs, trimmed
Juice of 1 lime
1 handful coriander (cilantro) leaves, chopped
Steamed rice, to serve
Thinly sliced spring onion (scallion), to serve

1. In a small food processor, add the lemongrass, shallot, ginger, lime leaves and garlic. Blend until almost a smooth paste.
2. Heat the olive oil and chilli crisp in a large deep saucepan over medium heat. Add the lemongrass mixture and cook for 2–3 minutes or until lightly softened.
3. Stir in the coconut milk, chicken stock, fish sauce, soy sauce and brown sugar. Place the chicken into the pot and cover with a lid. Cook for 15 minutes or until the chicken is completely cooked through. Remove the chicken, slice and return to the pot.
4. Divide steamed rice between bowls. Top with chicken and broth. Drizzle with the chilli oil and sprinkle with spring onion to serve.

Leah's notes This coconut chicken has our house in LOVE. Chilli crisp is an absolute favourite too. If you're buying a chilli oil, make sure to get one that is filled with the crispy bits!

Madras lentil curry

SERVES 6

PREP TIME 10 minutes

COOK TIME 35 minutes

Curries are such a 'me' meal, I could eat them for breakfast, lunch and dinner.

1 tablespoon olive oil
1 brown onion, finely diced
3 garlic cloves, crushed
1 tablespoon grated ginger
½ bunch coriander (cilantro), leaves picked and stems chopped
¼ cup (55 g) Madras curry paste
400 g (14 oz) tin chickpeas, drained and rinsed
1 cup (205 g) dry red lentils, rinsed
400 ml (14 fl oz) light coconut milk
2 cups (500 ml) vegetable stock
120 g (4¼ oz) baby spinach leaves
2–3 tablespoons lemon juice
Steamed basmati rice, to serve

1. Heat the olive oil in a small deep saucepan over medium heat.
2. Add the onion, garlic, ginger and coriander stems and cook for 2–3 minutes or until the onion is soft and translucent.
3. Add the curry paste and cook for around 1 minute or until fragrant. Add the chickpeas and lentils and stir to combine.
4. Stir in the coconut milk and vegetable stock. Reduce the heat to low and simmer for 30 minutes or until the lentils are tender.
5. When the lentils are tender, stir in the baby spinach, coriander leaves and lemon juice. Once the leaves have wilted, serve with rice.

Leah's notes This recipe can be made and frozen in bulk. Freeze rice and curry in single-serve containers for an easy dinner.

CROFTON

Moroccan beef and rice

SERVES 4
PREP TIME 10 minutes
COOK TIME 20 minutes

When I'm in need of a quick meal, mince is just such an easy protein to cook. I always go for the extra lean mince for our dinners so it feels less greasy.

2 tablespoons sesame oil
1 brown onion, diced
2 spring onions (scallions), thinly sliced
2 garlic cloves, crushed
500 g (1 lb 2 oz) lean beef mince
10 string beans, halved
1 small broccoli head, cut into florets
¼ cup (60 ml) soy sauce
Juice of 1 lime
1 handful coriander (cilantro), to garnish
Steamed basmati rice, to serve

MOROCCAN SPICE MIX
2 teaspoons smoked paprika
¼ teaspoon cayenne pepper
½ teaspoon ground cumin
½ teaspoon ground ginger
¼ teaspoon ground cloves

1. To make the Moroccan spice mix, combine all the ingredients in a small bowl.
2. Heat the sesame oil in a large wok or frying pan over medium heat. Once hot, add the onion, spring onion, spice mix and garlic and cook for 2–3 minutes or until the onion becomes translucent.
3. Add the mince and use a spatula to break it into smaller pieces. Cook for 6–8 minutes or until almost cooked through. Add the beans and broccoli. Cook for a further 2–3 minutes or until the veggies are tender.
4. Add the soy sauce and lime juice to the mixture and mix well. Garnish with coriander.
5. Serve with steamed rice.

Leah's notes This is a perfect meal prep recipe. Place into single-serve containers and freeze for a quick dinner or take-to-work lunch.

Honey and miso chicken traybake

SERVES 4
PREP TIME 10 minutes
COOK TIME 35 minutes

One-tray bakes are a dream! I'm always looking for something that's quick and easy at night, because we're all so busy, so a throw-together meal is the best.

4 large skin-on boneless chicken thighs, trimmed
10 baby potatoes, halved
1 bunch (about 150 g/5½ oz) asparagus
1 bunch (about 150 g/5½ oz) broccolini
Steamed basmati rice or a mixed salad, to serve

HONEY-MISO PASTE

1 tablespoon white miso paste
2 tablespoons sesame oil
2 garlic cloves, crushed
2 cm (¾ in) knob of ginger, grated
2 spring onions (scallions), thinly sliced
2 teaspoons gochujang or chilli paste
2 tablespoons honey
2 tablespoons water

1. Preheat the oven to 180°C (350°F) fan-forced. Line a large baking tray with baking paper.
2. To make the honey-miso paste, combine all the ingredients in a bowl and mix well.
3. Place the chicken thighs and potatoes into the prepared baking tray. Pour over three-quarters of the miso mixture and toss to coat. If you have time, you can leave this to marinate in the fridge for as long as you can before cooking.
4. Bake for 15 minutes. Add the asparagus and broccolini and the remaining miso mixture then toss to coat, and bake for a further 20 minutes or until the chicken is browned and cooked through. Serve with rice or a salad.

Leah's notes This is a perfect meal prep recipe, but also, the chicken is great for leftovers! Throw it into a wrap, pies or a salad.

CHAPTER
3

ONE MEAL INTO MANY

This chapter is hands-down my *favourite* way to cook. Make one thing, and turn it into a bunch of different meals (hello, organisation!). You might cook up a batch of meatballs, and one night you're having spaghetti and meatballs, the next it's meatloaf, then you might flatten them into little patties for burgers.

It's about making one base recipe, and flipping it into three completely different meals. You're never bored, but you're also not creating something from scratch each night. And that's a win in my book.

Herby roast chicken with rosemary + lemon

p 96

Leftover chicken pie

A comforting winter warmer just right for eating on the couch

p 97

Barbecue chicken pizza

A delicious pizza topping with spicy barbecue sauce

p 97

Orzo Greek chicken salad

An easy lunch on the go that's delicious served hot or cold

Delicious herby chicken is so versatile: enjoy it as a Sunday roast, then turn the leftovers into a hearty chicken pie, a barbecue pizza topping or a protein-packed Greek salad.

MAIN RECIPE

Herby roast chicken with rosemary and lemon

SERVES 4

PREP TIME 10 minutes

COOK TIME 1.5 hours

The herbed butter creates the juiciest chicken, which we love to cook up for a wholesome Sunday night dinner.

1.5 kg (3 lb 5 oz) whole chicken
2 tablespoons olive oil
Juice and zest of 1 lemon
½ cup (125 ml) chicken stock

HERBED BUTTER
3 garlic cloves, crushed
150 g (5½ oz) unsalted butter, at room temperature
4 large sage leaves, finely chopped
1 tablespoon fresh rosemary, finely chopped
1 tablespoon smoked paprika
1 tablespoon dried oregano
1 tablespoon salt
1 tablespoon freshly ground black pepper

1. Preheat the oven to 180°C (350°F) fan-forced. Trim any excess fat from the chicken (if you buy the chicken from a butcher you can usually skip this).
2. To make the herbed butter, mix all the ingredients in a bowl until well combined.
3. Carefully lifting and separating the skin, push one-quarter of the herbed butter underneath the skin of each breast.
4. Rub the olive oil over the chicken, then sprinkle the lemon juice and lemon zest all over. Rub the remaining herbed butter over the chicken.
5. Place the chicken into a roasting pan breast-side down and pour in the chicken stock. Cover with foil or a lid and roast for 1 hour.
6. Uncover, flip the chicken over so the breast is facing up, and roast for a further 30 minutes or until cooked through.
7. Shred the leftover chicken meat and keep in an airtight container in the fridge for meals throughout the week.

Leah's notes You can make the herbed butter ahead of time and refrigerate in an airtight container to make this recipe even quicker.

Leftover chicken pie

SERVES 4 **PREP TIME** 8 minutes **COOK TIME** 40 minutes

- 1 tablespoon olive oil
- 1 medium brown onion, finely diced
- 2 garlic cloves, crushed
- 1 teaspoon thyme leaves, chopped
- 2 cups (180 g) sliced mushrooms
- 8 asparagus spears, sliced into 2 cm (¾ in) pieces
- ¼ cup (15 g) chopped chives
- ⅓ cup (85 g) sour cream
- 2 cups (500 ml) chicken stock
- 500 g (1 lb 2 oz) shredded leftover roast chicken (see page 95)
- 2 tablespoons cornflour (cornstarch)
- 2 tablespoons water
- 1 egg, whisked
- 1 sheet puff pastry, thawed, cut 1 cm (½ in) larger than dish/dishes
- 2 teaspoons sesame seeds
- Sea salt flakes, for sprinkling

1. Preheat the oven to 180°C (350°F) fan-forced .
2. Heat the olive oil in a large saucepan over medium heat, then cook the onion, garlic and thyme for 2–3 minutes or until softened. Season with salt and freshly ground black pepper.
3. Add the mushrooms, asparagus and chives and cook for 10 minutes or until the vegetables have softened.
4. Stir in the sour cream, chicken stock and shredded chicken and cook for 10 minutes over low heat. Taste and season again with salt and pepper.
5. Mix the cornflour and water in a small bowl and stir into the chicken mixture. Cook for 5 minutes or until thickened.
6. Fill a large pie dish or four ramekins with the chicken mixture.
7. Brush the rim with egg and top with pastry. Press the edges down to seal.
8. Brush the pastry with more egg and sprinkle with sesame seeds and sea salt. Cut a few small slits in the top to allow steam to escape.
9. Bake for 25 minutes or until the pastry is puffed and golden.

Leah's notes Adding sesame seeds to the pastry not only makes it look delicious, but adds great flavour too.

Barbecue chicken pizza

SERVES 2 **PREP TIME** 8 minutes **COOK TIME** 15 minutes

1 tablespoon olive oil, plus extra to drizzle
2 button mushrooms, sliced
½ capsicum (pepper), finely chopped
¼ red onion, finely diced
2 pita breads
¼ cup (60 g) spicy barbecue sauce
1 cup (150 g) shredded leftover roast chicken (see page 95)
1 slice tinned pineapple, chopped
Grated mozzarella cheese (as much as you desire!)
Baby rocket (arugula), to serve (optional)

1. Preheat the oven to 180°C (350°F) fan-forced. Line a baking tray with baking paper.
2. Heat the olive oil in a small frying pan over medium heat. Cook the mushroom, capsicum and red onion for 5 minutes or until softened. Season with salt and freshly ground black pepper and set aside to cool slightly.
3. Heat a large frying pan over medium heat and toast the pita breads for 1–2 minutes each side or until lightly toasted. Transfer to the baking tray.
4. Top the pita breads with some barbecue sauce, chicken, pineapple, cooked mushroom mix and the cheese. Bake for 10 minutes or until golden and melted.
5. Top with fresh rocket (if using) drizzled with olive oil and a pinch of salt to serve.

Orzo Greek chicken salad

SERVES 2 **PREP TIME** 10 minutes **COOK TIME** 5 minutes

¼ cup (50 g) risoni (orzo)
1 cup (150 g) cherry tomatoes, halved
1 Lebanese (short) cucumber, sliced into rounds
1 small red capsicum (pepper), thinly sliced
½ red onion, sliced
½ × 400 g (14 oz) tin four bean mix, drained and rinsed
5–8 pitted kalamata olives
Small crumble of feta
1 cup (150 g) shredded leftover roast chicken (see page 95)
Lemon juice, dried oregano and olive oil, for dressing

1. Cook the risoni according to the packet instructions. Drain and set aside.
2. Mix the cherry tomatoes, cucumber, capsicum, red onion, four bean mix, olives and feta in a large bowl until combined.
3. Add the cooked risoni, shredded chicken, lemon juice, dried oregano, salt and a drizzle of olive oil. Gently toss to combine.

Leah's notes Swap the risoni for microwavable brown rice cups to make this meal even quicker.

Chicken schnitzels

p 102

Schnitzel burgers

A fast and tasty weeknight treat

p 102

Chicken katsu rice bowls

When I made this for Mitch, he asked me to marry him (again!)

p 103

Chicken parmigiana

Impress the family with a classic parmy

While they're delicious on their own, schnitties work on so many levels. Transform them into mouth-watering burgers, quick and easy chicken katsu rice bowls and pub-worthy chicken parmigiana.

MAIN RECIPE

Chicken schnitzels

MAKES 8

PREP TIME 20–30 minutes, plus chilling

COOK TIME 20 minutes

Chicken schnitzels are a family favourite, and this version has a medley of spices that give them a beautiful golden colour.

4 boneless, skinless chicken breasts
2 eggs
Juice and zest of 1 lemon
3 cups (180 g) panko breadcrumbs
1 tablespoon salt
1 tablespoon freshly ground black pepper
1 tablespoon dried oregano
1 tablespoon smoked paprika
1 tablespoon garlic powder
⅓ cup (80 ml) olive oil

1. Thinly slice each chicken breast horizontally into two schnitzels.
2. Whisk the eggs, lemon juice and lemon zest together in a shallow bowl.
3. Mix the breadcrumbs, salt, pepper, oregano, paprika and garlic powder together in a separate shallow bowl.
4. Dip each piece of chicken into the egg mixture, then into the breadcrumb mixture, pressing the breadcrumbs to ensure they stick. Transfer to a lined baking tray with baking paper between the layers. Refrigerate for 30 minutes. (You can store the uncooked schnitzels in the fridge in an airtight container for 2–3 days, or in the freezer for up to 1 month.)
5. When ready to cook, heat the olive oil in a frying pan over medium heat. Cook the schnitzels in batches for 5-10 minutes each side or until golden brown and cooked through. Transfer to a plate lined with paper towel to drain. Once cool, refrigerate in an airtight container and use within 2–3 days.

Leah's notes You can make the crumb mix ahead of time by combining the breadcrumbs and spices. This stores well in an airtight container in the pantry.

Schnitzel burgers

SERVES 4 **PREP TIME** 5 minutes **COOK TIME** 10 minutes

- 4–6 cooked chicken schnitzels (see page 101)
- 4 burger buns
- 4 slices tasty or burger cheese
- 1 cup (90 g) shredded iceberg lettuce
- 1 small tomato, sliced
- 5–8 burger pickles
- Kewpie mayo, or sauce of your choice

1. Reheat the schnitzels in the oven or microwave.
2. To assemble, split the buns and then toast them. Top each base with a chicken schnitzel, cheese, lettuce, tomato, burger pickles and sauce of your choice. Finish with the bun tops.

Leah's notes Lightly melt the cheese over the schnitzel before assembling to make this extra delicious.

Chicken katsu rice bowls

SERVES 2 **PREP TIME** 10 minutes **COOK TIME** 10 minutes

- 2 cooked chicken schnitzels (see page 101)
- ½ cup (80 g) frozen edamame beans
- 1 teaspoon soy sauce
- 2 cups (370 g) cooked rice
- 1 small cucumber, sliced into rounds
- ½ avocado, thinly sliced
- Spicy mayo, or sauce of your choice
- 1 spring onion (scallion), sliced
- Toasted sesame seeds, to serve

1. Reheat the schnitzels in the oven or microwave.
2. Heat the edamame beans and soy sauce in a small saucepan over medium heat for 2–3 minutes or until warmed through. Season with salt and freshly ground black pepper.
3. Slice the chicken schnitzel into strips.
4. Divide the rice between bowls. Top with sliced schnitzel.
5. Add the cucumber, avocado and edamame beans to each bowl. Drizzle with spicy mayo and sprinkle with spring onion and sesame seeds to serve.

Leah's notes I'm a lover of all things Kewpie, that's my mayo of choice!

Chicken parmigiana

SERVES 4 **PREP TIME** 10 minutes **COOK TIME** 10 minutes (or 45 minutes if making sauce from scratch)

2 cups (500 g) napoletana sauce (store-bought or see below for a DIY version)
8 cooked chicken schnitzels (see page 101)
1 cup (130 g) grated mozzarella cheese

NAPOLETANA SAUCE

2 tablespoons olive oil
1 medium brown onion, finely diced
4 garlic cloves, crushed
1 red chilli, deseeded and finely sliced
2 tablespoons tomato paste (concentrated purée)
1 tablespoon dried oregano
1 teaspoon ground allspice
1 cinnamon stick
800 g (1 lb 12 oz) tin crushed tomatoes
5–8 fresh basil leaves

1. Preheat the oven to 180°C (350°F) fan-forced. Line a baking tray with baking paper.
2. To make the sauce, heat the olive oil in a small saucepan over medium heat. Cook the onion, garlic and chilli, stirring, for 5 minutes or until the onion becomes translucent.
3. Stir in the tomato paste, oregano, allspice and cinnamon stick. Season with salt and freshly ground black pepper. Cook for 2 minutes or until slightly darkened. Add the crushed tomatoes and cook for 5 minutes. Taste here and season with salt and pepper. Reduce the heat to low and simmer for 20 minutes, adding the basil in the last minute of cooking. Remove the cinnamon stick before using.
4. Place the cooked schnitzels on the baking tray. Top each with napoletana sauce and cheese.
5. Bake for 10 minutes or until completely warmed through and the cheese is melted.

Spicy beef ragu

p 108

Ragu with cheesy garlic mash

Turn a side into a meal with this perfect combo

p 108

Ragu with spiced rice

This aromatic rice dish is light and hearty all at once

p 109

Beef lasagne

Serve this and watch everyone come back for seconds

There's nothing quite like a slow-cooked ragu to add depth of flavour to all sorts of dishes. Try it with cheesy garlic mash, aromatic spiced rice or in my must-try lasagne.

MAIN RECIPE

Spicy beef ragu

SERVES 4
PREP TIME 10 minutes
COOK TIME 2.5 hours

This spicy beef ragu is on weekly rotation in my house. The meat is super tender and the cinnamon adds so much warmth.

¼ cup (60 ml) olive oil
1.5 kg (3 lb 5 oz) oyster blade steak, cut into bite-sized pieces
1 large brown onion, finely diced
5–7 garlic cloves, crushed
1 long red chilli, finely diced
¼ cup (60 g) tomato paste (concentrated purée)
2 teaspoons dried oregano
1 teaspoon ground allspice
2 cinnamon sticks
2 bay leaves
2 cups (500 ml) beef stock
3 × 400 g (14 oz) tins chopped tomatoes
Parmesan cheese rinds (optional)
1 handful basil leaves, to serve

1. Heat a generous drizzle of olive oil in a large pot or slow cooker over medium-high heat. Cook the beef, in batches, for 15 minutes or until lightly browned all over. Season each batch with salt and freshly ground black pepper and add more oil as necessary. Transfer to a plate.
2. Drizzle a touch more olive oil into the same pot and reduce the heat to medium. Add the onion and cook for 2–3 minutes or until softened.
3. Add the garlic and chilli and cook for a further 1 minute. Add the tomato paste, oregano, allspice, cinnamon and bay leaves and cook, stirring, for 2–3 minutes or until fragrant. Season with salt and pepper.
4. Add the beef stock and chopped tomatoes and bring to a simmer. Return the beef to the pot and add the parmesan rinds (if using). Simmer, covered, for 2 hours. If using a slow cooker, cook on high for 4 hours, or 8 hours on low.
5. Once the sauce has cooked for the set time, you can uncover and cook it down, depending on the thickness you prefer.
6. Discard the cinnamon sticks and parmesan rinds. Serve topped with fresh basil leaves.

Leah's notes Taking the time to brown the meat in batches adds a lot of flavour to this meal.

Ragu with cheesy garlic mash

SERVES 2 **PREP TIME** 5 minutes **COOK TIME** 25 minutes

4 large white mashing potatoes, peeled and halved
1 garlic clove, crushed
2 tablespoons (40 g) butter
2 tablespoons thickened (heavy/pouring) cream
¼ cup (25 g) grated cheddar cheese
1 teaspoon fresh chives, finely chopped
2 cups leftover spicy beef ragu (see page 107), warmed

1. Bring a deep pot of salted water to the boil. Add the potatoes and cook for 15 minutes or until tender and cooked through. Drain and return to the pot.
2. Mash the potatoes with the garlic, butter, thickened cream, cheese and chives while they're hot so everything melts together. Season with salt and freshly ground black pepper.
3. Serve with leftover ragu.

Leah's notes A mix of cheddar and parmesan cheeses would go beautifully here.

Ragu with spiced rice

SERVES 2 **PREP TIME** 5 minutes **COOK TIME** 20 minutes

1 tablespoon (20 g) butter
½ small brown onion, finely diced
2 whole allspice
3 whole cloves
1 cup basmati rice, washed
2 cups (500 ml) beef stock
3 cups leftover spicy beef ragu (see page 107), warmed
Grated parmesan cheese and basil leaves, to serve

1. Melt the butter in a small saucepan over medium-high heat.
2. Add the onion, allspice and cloves and cook for 2–3 minutes or until the onion has softened.
3. Add the washed rice and beef stock and cover with a lid. When the mixture comes to the boil, reduce the heat to a low simmer and cover. Cook for 15 minutes then remove from the heat and set aside, covered, for 5 minutes.
4. Serve the rice with leftover ragu and a sprinkle of grated parmesan and basil leaves.

Leah's notes No beef stock at home? A vegetable stock would work well here too.

Beef lasagne

SERVES 4 **PREP TIME** 20 minutes **COOK TIME** 40 minutes

1 batch spicy beef ragu (see page 107)
16 lasagne sheets (or more depending on size of tray)
3 cups (390 g) grated mozzarella
1 cup (100 g) grated parmesan cheese
1 large handful fresh basil leaves

1. Preheat the oven to 180°C (350°F) fan-forced.
2. In a deep baking dish, layer the ragu with lasagne sheets, cheese and a sprinkle of basil leaves.
3. Create 4–5 layers, finishing with a layer of sauce topped with a layer of cheese.
4. Cover with foil and bake for 40 minutes. Uncover for the last few minutes of baking for the cheese to get golden. Remove from the oven and set aside to rest in the dish for 10 minutes.
5. Serve with more fresh basil on top.

Leah's notes Either fresh or dried lasagne sheets can be used in this recipe.

Simple meatballs with extra veggies

p 114

Meatloaf with mashed potato

A different take, and a match made in heaven

p 115

Beef burgers

Go for patties and serve with pickles and cheese for the ultimate burger

p 115

Spaghetti and meatballs

Always a winner, either with napoletana sauce from scratch or store-bought

One meatball recipe, four dinners! Enjoy these on their own or transform this veggie-packed mince into a spaghetti dish, burgers or a classic meatloaf.

MAIN RECIPE

Simple meatballs with extra veggies

MAKES 30 meatballs
PREP TIME 15 minutes
COOK TIME 10 minutes

I love making these meatballs when I want to sneak some extra veggies in. There's no need to roll all the mixture into balls if you're making the burgers or meatloaf recipes.

1 kg (2 lb 4 oz) beef mince (or pork or lamb)
1 small zucchini (courgette), finely grated and excess moisture squeezed out
1 small carrot, finely grated and excess moisture squeezed out
2 button mushrooms, finely chopped
1 brown onion, finely diced
3 garlic cloves, crushed
½ bunch fresh parsley, finely chopped
1 tablespoon dried oregano
2 eggs
½ cup (55 g) fine breadcrumbs
Olive oil, for cooking

1. Place the beef mince, vegetables, garlic, parsley, oregano, eggs and breadcrumbs in a large mixing bowl. Season with salt and freshly ground black pepper and mix well with your hands.
2. Using around 1 tablespoon at a time, roll into 30 balls. These can be frozen at this point if you prefer, or they can be frozen once cooked.
3. Heat a generous drizzle of olive oil in a large frying pan over medium heat.
4. Cook the meatballs in batches, adding extra oil as necessary, for 4–5 minutes or until browned and cooked through.

Leah's notes It's worth taking the time to squeeze out the excess moisture in the veggies – this will ensure your meatballs don't fall apart when cooking.

Meatloaf with mashed potato

SERVES 4 **PREP TIME** 5 minutes **COOK TIME** 1 hour

1½ tablespoons Worcestershire sauce
2 teaspoons mustard
1 cup (250 g) tomato passata (puréed tomatoes)
2 teaspoons apple cider vinegar
4 tablespoons beef stock
2 tablespoons tomato paste (concentrated purée)
½ teaspoon cayenne pepper
700 g (1 lb 9 oz) leftover meatball mixture (see page 113)
4 large white mashing potatoes, peeled and cut in half
3 tablespoons (60 g) butter
2 teaspoons garlic salt

1. Preheat the oven to 180°C (350°F) fan-forced. Line a loaf tin with baking paper or spray with olive oil.
2. Combine the Worcestershire sauce, mustard, tomato passata, apple cider vinegar, beef stock, tomato paste and cayenne pepper in a bowl.
3. Press the leftover meatball mixture into the loaf tin and pour the red sauce over the top.
4. Cover with foil and bake for 30 minutes. Remove the foil and bake for a further 20 minutes or until browned and cooked through.
5. Meanwhile, make the mash. Bring a deep pot of salted water to the boil. Add the potatoes and boil until completely cooked through. Drain and transfer back to the pot. Add the butter and garlic salt and mash until smooth.
6. Slice the meatloaf and serve with mashed potatoes.

Leah's notes Add a side of steamed frozen vegetables for a quick and easy addition to the meal.

Beef burgers

SERVES 4 **PREP TIME** 10 minutes **COOK TIME** 15 minutes

400 g (14 oz) leftover meatball mixture (see page 113)
1 tablespoon olive oil
1 brown onion, sliced into rings
4 burger buns, halved
4 slices tasty or burger cheese
1 cup shredded iceberg lettuce
1 tomato, thinly sliced
8 burger pickles
Sauces, to serve (Kewpie mayo, tomato, mustard!)

1. Instead of rolling the mixture into meatballs, roll it into large balls using about 100 g (3½ oz) mixture per burger and flatten each into a patty.
2. Heat a small drizzle of olive oil in a frying pan and cook the onions with a pinch of salt for 8–10 minutes or until caramelised.
3. In another frying pan or on a barbecue, heat a drizzle of olive oil and cook the patties for 2–3 minutes on each side or until browned and cooked through.
4. Toast the buns and add a patty and some cheese, onion, lettuce, tomato and burger pickles to each. Serve with sauces of your choice.

Spaghetti and meatballs

SERVES 4 **PREP TIME** 10 minutes **COOK TIME** 30 minutes

4 cups (1 kg) napoletana sauce (store-bought or made from scratch, see page 103)
16 leftover meatballs, cooked or raw (see page 113)
400 g (14 oz) spaghetti

1. Gently heat the napoletana sauce in a saucepan.
2. Add the meatballs to the sauce and simmer for 20 minutes or until heated through or fully cooked.
3. Meanwhile, cook the pasta according to the packet instructions. Serve with the meatballs and sauce.

Leah's notes Using good-quality tinned tomatoes is the secret to a delicious homemade napoletana sauce – look for one with a higher percentage of tomatoes instead of tomato juice.

Steak with baked vegetables

p 120

Mexican-style rice bowl

Loaded with colourful and nutritious ingredients

p 120

Steak sandwich

Upgrade your steak sandwich with chimichurri – it packs in so much flavour!

p 121

Steak fajita bowls

A colourful crisp combo, with a twist of lime

Flip leftover grilled steak into a Mexican-style rice bowl, a luxe steak sandwich or a spicy fajita bowl.

MAIN RECIPE

Steak with baked vegetables

SERVES 2
PREP TIME 10 minutes
COOK TIME 30 minutes

Steak and vegetables is such an easy dinner. Roasting the veggies creates a depth of flavour and texture, while the fresh lemon really brings it all together.

2 × 300 g (10½ oz) sirloin steaks
2 white potatoes, cut into cubes
1 red onion, cut into wedges
2 carrots, sliced into thick rounds
½ broccoli head, cut into florets
Olive oil, for drizzling
Pinch of dried oregano, plus extra to season
Juice of ½ lemon

1. Preheat the oven to 180°C (350°F) fan-forced. Remove the steaks from the fridge about 30 minutes before cooking so they can come to room temperature.
2. Place the potato, red onion, carrot and broccoli in a large baking dish. Drizzle with olive oil and season with oregano, salt and freshly ground black pepper. Squeeze the lemon juice over the top, toss to combine and roast for 30 minutes, tossing occasionally.
3. Drizzle the steaks with olive oil and season with salt, pepper and oregano on both sides.
4. When the veggies are almost ready, heat a cast-iron frying pan or barbecue over medium heat.
5. Cook the steak for 2½–3 minutes each side for medium or until cooked to your liking. Remove from the pan and set aside to rest.
6. Slice the steak and serve with the vegetables.

Leah's notes Allowing your steak to rest for a few minutes before serving helps keep it juicy and cooked to perfection.

Mexican-style rice bowl

SERVES 2 **PREP TIME** 10 minutes **COOK TIME** 30 minutes

1 small sweet potato, peeled and cut into cubes
Olive oil, for drizzling
½ × 400 g (14 oz) tin corn kernels, drained and rinsed
½ × 400 g (14 oz) tin black beans, drained and rinsed
2 tablespoons taco seasoning
2 leftover cooked steaks (see page 119), thinly sliced
1 cup (185 g) cooked brown rice
1 handful mixed salad leaves
½ avocado, thinly sliced
¼ red onion, finely diced
6 cherry tomatoes
Sriracha or Kewpie mayo, to serve

1. Preheat the oven to 180°C (350°F) fan-forced. Line a baking tray with baking paper.
2. Place the sweet potato on the baking tray and drizzle with olive oil. Season with salt and freshly ground black pepper. Roast for 30 minutes, or until softened.
3. Meanwhile, heat a frying pan over medium heat with a drizzle of olive oil. Cook the corn kernels and black beans for 4–5 minutes or until heated through. Season with half the taco seasoning. Transfer to a bowl.
4. Return the pan to medium heat and warm the steak until heated through. Season with the remaining taco seasoning.
5. Divide the brown rice between two bowls. Top with the mixed leaves, sweet potato, corn mixture, steak, avocado, red onion and cherry tomatoes. Serve with sauce, if desired.

Leah's notes This dish would be great served with some crunchy pita chips on the side and a squeeze of fresh lime.

Steak sandwich

SERVES 1 **PREP TIME** 10 minutes **COOK TIME** 25 minutes

1 handful frozen fries
2 slices sourdough bread
1 leftover cooked steak (see page 119), thinly sliced
2 tablespoons chimichurri
1 tablespoon aioli
1 handful shredded iceberg lettuce

1. Cook the fries according to the packet instructions, in the oven or air fryer.
2. Toast the bread in the toaster or under the grill and warm the steak, if desired.
3. Spread the chimichurri on one slice of the toasted bread, and spread aioli on the other slice.
4. Add the steak and lettuce to the bread and top with fries. Sandwich together and cut in half to serve.

Leah's notes Swap sourdough for Turkish bread if desired.

Steak fajita bowls

SERVES 2 **PREP TIME** 10 minutes **COOK TIME** 10 minutes

Olive oil, for drizzling
¼ small red onion, cut into thin wedges
½ small red capsicum (pepper), thinly sliced
½ small green capsicum (pepper), thinly sliced
2 garlic cloves, crushed
½ teaspoon paprika
½ teaspoon chilli powder
2 teaspoons ground cumin
1 leftover cooked steak (see page 119), thinly sliced
30 g (1 oz) mixed salad leaves
¼ cup (40 g) tinned black beans, drained and rinsed
¼ medium avocado, sliced
Spicy Kewpie mayo, to serve
1 small handful fresh coriander (cilantro) leaves
Lime juice, to taste

1. Heat a drizzle of olive oil in a frying pan over medium heat. Cook the onion, capsicum, garlic, paprika, chilli powder and cumin for 5–7 minutes or until the veggies begin to soften. Add the sliced steak and toss to warm through. Season with salt and freshly ground black pepper.
2. Divide the mixed leaves between two bowls. Top with steak and capsicum mixture, black beans, avocado and a drizzle of Kewpie mayo.
3. Sprinkle with fresh coriander and a big squeeze of lime to serve.

Leah's notes You can add in some rice of your choice to bulk up this meal.

Thai barbecue chicken skewers

p 126

Thai chicken and rice bowls

Bonus points for the ribboned veggies; they make this look very impressive with such little effort

p 126

Chicken ice-cube sushi

See my hack for making sushi, leaving you with more time to enjoy the flavourful filling

p 127

Greek chicken salad

The creaminess of the feta and the salty olives pack in so much deliciousness; I could eat this every day!

This flavour-packed chicken also works brilliantly in a rice bowl with ribboned veggies, thinly sliced in ice-cube sushi or popped into a Greek chicken salad, for a cross-cultural flavour bomb.

MAIN RECIPE

Thai barbecue chicken skewers

SERVES 4
PREP TIME 10 minutes
COOK TIME 10 minutes

These Thai chicken skewers are perfect to bring to a barbecue; the curry paste adds a tasty kick and helps get a beautiful char on the meat.

1 tablespoon red curry paste
1 teaspoon cracked black pepper
2 tablespoons soy sauce
1 tablespoon ground turmeric
5 coriander (cilantro) roots, finely diced
4 garlic cloves, crushed
¼ cup (60 ml) tinned coconut milk
1 kg (2 lb 4 oz) boneless, skinless chicken thighs, cut into bite-sized pieces

1. Soak 12 wooden skewers in cold water to stop them from burning while cooking.
2. Combine the red curry paste, pepper, soy sauce, turmeric, coriander roots, garlic and coconut milk in a large bowl.
3. Add the chicken thighs and mix well to coat completely with the marinade.
4. Marinate in the fridge for as long as you can (overnight is awesome) but if you don't have the time, skewer right away.
5. Using one skewer at a time, take pieces of the chicken and skewer all the way through until you reach the top. Continue until you have used up all the chicken. You can make these little cocktail skewers, or more hearty larger ones.
6. Heat a barbecue or chargrill pan over medium-high heat. Grill the chicken on all sides for about 10 minutes or until fully cooked through.
7. Serve with salad for a meal, or pass around as an appetiser.

Leah's notes Swap the chicken thighs for breast if you prefer – pork works nicely with this recipe too!

Thai chicken and rice bowls

SERVES 2 **PREP TIME** 10 minutes **COOK TIME** 25 minutes

1 tablespoon (20 g) butter
½ brown onion, finely diced
1 cup (200 g) basmati rice
2 cups (500 ml) chicken stock
4 leftover Thai barbecue chicken skewers (see page 125)
1 cucumber, peeled into ribbons
1 carrot, peeled into ribbons
2 tablespoons pickled red onions
Spicy Kewpie mayo, for drizzling

1. In a small saucepan with a lid, melt the butter over medium heat. Cook the brown onion for 2 minutes or until beginning to soften.
2. Add the basmati rice and chicken stock and stir to combine.
3. Cover with a lid and bring to the boil. Reduce the heat to a low simmer and cook for 15 minutes. Remove from the heat and leave to stand, covered, for 5 minutes.
4. Heat the leftover chicken. Divide the rice between bowls. Top with the chicken skewers, cucumber, carrot, pickled onions and a big squeeze of spicy Kewpie mayo.

Leah's notes To make a super quick pickle, add thinly sliced red onion to a bowl with a few tablespoons of vinegar and allow to sit while you prep everything else.

Chicken ice-cube sushi

SERVES 2 **PREP TIME** 10 minutes **CHILL TIME** 15 minutes

1 cup (210 g) sushi rice, cooked
2 leftover Thai barbecue chicken skewers (see page 125), chopped into small pieces
½ avocado, thinly sliced
Kewpie mayonnaise, optional
1 teaspoon furikake
Soy sauce, to serve

1. Line a large silicone ice-cube tray with plastic wrap. Try to push the plastic wrap into each hole of the tray, creating a layer all around it so it's super easy to pop out.
2. Press a little rice into each hole of the tray and then layer with chicken, avocado, Kewpie (if using), furikake and more rice to enclose. Press down firmly to ensure it all stays inside.
3. Cover with another layer of plastic wrap and place in the fridge for 15 minutes to set. Pop out of the tray by lifting the plastic wrap up.
4. Serve with soy sauce.

Leah's notes If you don't have furikake, some toasted sesame seeds mixed with some finely chopped seaweed sheets would be delicious.

Greek chicken salad

SERVES 2 **PREP TIME** 10 minutes **COOK TIME** Nil

4 leftover Thai barbecue chicken skewers (see page 125)
4–5 cherry tomatoes, halved
1 Lebanese (short) cucumber, sliced into rounds
½ red onion, thinly sliced
4 cm (1½ in) piece feta cheese, crumbled
4–6 pitted kalamata olives
1 small handful baby rocket (arugula)
Olive oil, for drizzling
Lemon juice, to taste

1. Warm the leftover chicken skewers.
2. Combine the cherry tomatoes, cucumber, red onion, feta cheese, olives and rocket in a large bowl.
3. Add the chicken, a drizzle of olive oil, a squeeze of lemon juice and a pinch of salt. Toss to combine.
4. Taste and season if necessary before serving.

Leah's notes I love to dress this salad just before serving to keep everything crunchy and fresh. Don't skip the salt – it helps bring all the flavours together, I promise!

Chilli garlic prawns

p 132

Creamy garlic prawns

Cook the prawns in coconut milk and veg for a silky meal

p 132

Prawn and pumpkin risoni

The world is your oyster here as you can add loads of different veg to this risoni

p 133

Napoletana with prawns

A homemade napoletana with spicy prawns and pasta – yes please!

These spicy garlic prawns are delicious as the main event, plus you can turn them into a creamy coconut bowl, a hearty risoni or a fragrant napoletana sauce with pasta.

MAIN RECIPE

Chilli garlic prawns

SERVES 6 (as a starter)
PREP TIME 10 minutes
COOK TIME 5–10 minutes

These garlic prawns are such a winner in our house! The chilli garlic butter works just as well with chicken, too.

500 g (1 lb 2 oz) raw banana prawns, peeled and deveined, tails on
2 tablespoons olive oil
2 tablespoons fresh flat-leaf parsley, finely chopped
1 red chilli, finely chopped
4 garlic cloves, crushed
½ teaspoon smoked paprika
3 tablespoons (60 g) butter

1. Combine the prawns, olive oil, parsley, chilli, garlic and paprika in a large bowl. Season with salt and freshly ground black pepper. Toss well until evenly coated.
2. Heat the butter in a large frying pan over medium-low heat.
3. Add the prawns in a single layer and cook for 2–3 minutes each side, or until lightly golden and just cooked through.
4. Transfer to a serving plate and serve immediately.

Leah's notes You could freeze the prawns uncooked, but marinated. This way, they're so easy to defrost and throw into the pan! No mess and no fuss.

Creamy garlic prawns

SERVES 4 **PREP TIME** 10 minutes **COOK TIME** 20 minutes

2 tablespoons olive oil
½ fresh long red chilli, deseeded and chopped
1 small handful flat-leaf parsley, finely chopped, plus extra to serve
1 small brown onion, finely diced
4 garlic cloves, crushed
400 ml (14 fl oz) tin coconut milk
1 cup (60 g) broccoli florets
10 snow peas, halved
4 white button mushrooms, quartered
20 leftover cooked garlic prawns (see page 131)
Lime juice, to serve
Basmati rice, to serve

1. Heat the olive oil in a large frying pan over medium–high heat. Add the chilli, parsley, onion and garlic. Cook, stirring, for 2 minutes or until fragrant and the onion begins to soften.
2. Pour in the coconut milk and bring to a gentle simmer.
3. Add the broccoli, snow peas and mushrooms. Simmer for 2–3 minutes or until the vegetables are lightly cooked but still have their texture.
4. Season with salt and freshly ground black pepper to taste. Stir in the leftover garlic prawns and cook for another 1–2 minutes or until heated through.
5. Garnish with extra parsley or a squeeze of lime if desired and serve over rice.

Leah's notes A little fish sauce in this mixture is a really good addition for a salty hidden flavour.

Prawn and pumpkin risoni

SERVES 4 **PREP TIME** 10 minutes **COOK TIME** 25 minutes

Olive oil, for cooking
1 brown onion, finely diced
1 cup (155 g) diced pumpkin
1 teaspoon fresh thyme
3 garlic cloves, crushed
Juice and zest of 1 lemon
⅔ cup (130 g) risoni (orzo)
3 cups (750 ml) vegetable stock
2 handfuls baby spinach
10 leftover cooked garlic prawns (see page 131)
100 g (3½ oz) feta cheese, crumbled

1. Heat a drizzle of olive oil in a deep pan over medium heat.
2. Add the onion, pumpkin and thyme. Cook for 5 minutes, or until the onion is soft and translucent and the pumpkin begins to soften.
3. Stir in the garlic, lemon zest and lemon juice. Cook for another 2 minutes until fragrant.
4. Add the risoni and pour in the vegetable stock. Simmer, stirring occasionally, for 10 minutes or until the risoni is tender. Season with salt and freshly ground black pepper to taste.
5. When the risoni is nearly done, stir through the spinach and allow it to wilt.
6. Add the leftover garlic prawns and warm through for 1–2 minutes. Remove from the heat and serve topped with crumbled feta.

Napoletana with prawns

SERVES 4 **PREP TIME** 10 minutes **COOK TIME** 30 minutes

Olive oil, for cooking
1 brown onion, finely diced
3 garlic cloves, crushed
½ long red chilli, finely diced
2 tablespoons tomato paste (concentrated purée)
1 tablespoon dried oregano
1 cinnamon stick
¼ cup (40 g) pitted kalamata olives
2 × 400 g (14 oz) tins crushed tomatoes
1 cup (250 ml) chicken stock
1 handful fresh basil leaves, plus extra to serve
20 leftover cooked garlic prawns (see page 131)
Cooked pasta, to serve

1. Heat a drizzle of olive oil in a deep pan over medium–high heat. Add the onion, garlic and chilli, and cook, stirring regularly, for 3–5 minutes, or until the onion is soft and translucent.
2. Stir in the tomato paste, oregano, cinnamon stick and olives. Season with salt and freshly ground black pepper. Cook for 2 minutes to allow the flavours to develop.
3. Pour in the crushed tomatoes and chicken stock. Bring to a simmer and cook for 15 minutes, stirring occasionally, until the sauce begins to thicken.
4. Add the basil leaves and simmer for another 5 minutes.
5. Once the sauce has thickened and is full of flavour, stir through the leftover garlic prawns and cook for 1–2 minutes until just heated through.
6. Serve hot over your favourite cooked pasta, and top with extra basil if desired.

Leah's notes I love serving this with crusty garlic bread for dipping!

Barbecue beef brisket

p 138

Barbecue beef brisket toasties

The brisket, sauce and cheesy pickle combo will have you dreaming about this all day

p 138

Barbecue beef brisket salad sandwich

Transform your salad sambo with this smoky treat

p 139

Barbecue beef brisket tacos

Win Taco Tuesday with this easy and delicious filling idea

This tender, smoky meat is even more delicious the next day – so put it to good use in toasties, sandwiches or tacos.

MAIN RECIPE

Barbecue beef brisket

SERVES 6

PREP TIME 15 minutes

COOK TIME 5 hours, plus 30 minutes resting

For so long it was my mission to create the perfect smoky barbecue spice blend, and let me tell you – this is it! Rubbed onto brisket, it creates a hearty and tender hunk of meat that is simply delicious.

1.5 kg (3 lb 5 oz) beef brisket, fat trimmed
Juice of 1 lemon

BARBECUE SPICE BLEND
¼ cup (60 ml) olive oil
1 tablespoon chipotle in adobo sauce
2 tablespoons brown sugar
1 tablespoon honey
2 tablespoons onion powder
2 teaspoons ground coriander
1 tablespoon garlic powder
2 teaspoons ground cumin
1 tablespoon smoked paprika
1 tablespoon salt

1. To make the spice blend, combine all the ingredients in a bowl and mix together well.
2. Preheat the oven to 140°C (275°F) fan-forced.
3. Place the brisket on a wire rack in a roasting pan. Rub the spice blend all over the brisket and leave to sit for 1 hour to marinate and come to room temperature, if possible.
4. Pour enough water into the roasting pan so that it almost touches the rack, but not the meat. Cover the pan tightly with foil and bake for 5 hours.
5. Remove from the oven and set aside to rest for at least 30 minutes. Slice and drizzle with lemon juice before serving.

Leah's notes Using smoked paprika is key to getting that smoky barbecue flavour.

Barbecue beef brisket toasties

SERVES 1 **PREP TIME** 10 minutes **COOK TIME** 5 minutes

1 tablespoon butter (20 g), plus extra for smearing
2 large slices white bread
2 slices leftover beef brisket (see page 137)
2 slices cheddar cheese
2 burger pickles
Barbecue sauce, for drizzling

1. Smear butter on each slice of bread from edge to edge. With the buttered side down, add the beef brisket, cheese, burger pickles and barbecue sauce to one piece of bread. Sandwich with the top piece, leaving the buttered side up.
2. Cook in a sandwich press or frying pan until the bread is golden brown and the cheese has melted.

Leah's notes This toastie is so good with a side of fresh slaw.

Barbecue beef brisket salad sandwich

SERVES 1 **PREP TIME** 5 minutes **COOK TIME** Nil

Whole-egg mayonnaise, for smearing
2 large slices sourdough bread
2 slices leftover beef brisket (see page 137)
2 slices cheddar cheese
½ carrot, grated
½ cucumber, sliced lengthways
4 tinned beetroot slices
2 thin tomato slices

1. Smear mayonnaise over the sourdough slices and top one slice with beef brisket, cheese, carrot, cucumber, beetroot and tomato. Season with salt and freshly ground black pepper.
2. Sandwich with the top piece of bread and slice in half.

Barbecue beef brisket tacos

SERVES 2 **PREP TIME** 5 minutes **COOK TIME** 5 minutes

4 mini tortillas
4 slices leftover beef brisket (see page 137)

TOPPING IDEAS

⅓ cup (75 g) guacamole
2 cups (145 g) shredded iceberg lettuce
½ medium tomato, diced
½ small jalapeño, sliced
1 lime, cut into wedges
Spicy Kewpie mayo

1. Heat the tortillas and the leftover brisket.
2. Top each tortilla with a smear of guac, then the brisket, lettuce, tomato, jalapeño, a squeeze of lime and a drizzle of Kewpie mayonnaise.

Leah's notes Some fresh coriander (cilantro) would go perfectly with these and add a pop of colour too!

Beef bolognese

p 144

Bolognese eggplant boats

My spin on eggplant parmigiana, with rich bolognese

p 144

Nachos

These hit the spot every time, especially with homemade guacamole

p 145

Loaded sweet potato

You'll love this hearty meal, with fresh salsa and sour cream

Bologneses surely holds the record for the most ways it can be reimagined: nachos is an easy win, but have you tried it on eggplant boats or a roasted sweet potato?

MAIN RECIPE

Beef bolognese

SERVES 6–8

PREP TIME 10 minutes

COOK TIME 50 minutes

The smell of this sauce cooking away always brings back the best memories. This is such a homely meal that the whole family loves.

1 tablespoon olive oil
1 large brown onion, finely diced
4–6 garlic cloves, crushed
1 long red chilli, thinly sliced
1 zucchini (courgette), grated
4 button mushrooms, grated
500 g (1 lb 2 oz) lean beef mince
2 tablespoons tomato paste (concentrated purée)
2 teaspoons mustard powder
1 tablespoon dried oregano
1 cinnamon stick
2 bay leaves
2 × 400 g (14 oz) tins crushed tomatoes
1 cup (250 ml) beef stock
½ cup (50 g) grated parmesan cheese
10 basil leaves, roughly chopped
Cooked pasta, to serve

1. Heat the olive oil in a large saucepan over medium-high heat. Add the onion, garlic and chilli and cook for 3–4 minutes or until the onion becomes translucent.
2. Add the zucchini and mushroom and cook for 6–8 minutes or until the liquid has evaporated.
3. Add the mince and cook, breaking it apart with a wooden spoon, for 5–6 minutes or until browned and all the liquid has evaporated. Add the tomato paste, mustard powder, oregano, cinnamon stick and bay leaves. Season with salt and freshly ground black pepper and cook, stirring, for 1 minute or until fragrant.
4. Stir in the crushed tomatoes and beef stock. Add the parmesan and stir to combine.
5. Cover with a lid and simmer for 30 minutes, stirring occasionally. Stir in the basil and serve with your favourite type of pasta.

Leah's notes This recipe can easily be doubled to feed a lot of people. This sauce freezes well, so it makes for a great meal prep option too.

Bologneese eggplant boats

SERVES 2 **PREP TIME** 5 minutes **COOK TIME** 30 minutes

2 eggplants (aubergines), sliced in half horizontally
Olive oil, for coating
2 ladles of bolognese sauce (see page 143)
2 tablespoons cottage cheese
1 small handful grated mozzarella cheese
1 tablespoon fresh parsley, finely chopped
Green salad or mashed potatoes, to serve

1. Preheat the oven to 200°C (400°F) fan-forced.
2. Slice a diamond pattern into the eggplant flesh, rub with olive oil and season with salt. Place on a baking tray.
3. Bake for 20–25 minutes or until softened.
4. Remove from the oven and ladle the bolognese sauce over each eggplant piece. Top with cottage cheese and mozzarella, then sprinkle with parsley. Return to the oven and bake until the cheese is melted, 5–10 minutes.
5. Serve with salad or mashed potatoes.

Leah's notes I love to cook these a little longer to get the cheese perfectly golden and a little crispy. Fresh basil can be used if you don't have parsley.

Nachos

SERVES 2 **PREP TIME** 10 minutes **COOK TIME** 10 minutes

1 avocado, mashed
1 garlic clove, crushed
1 teaspoon garlic salt
Juice of 1 lemon
2 ladles of bolognese sauce (see page 143)
½ × 400 g (14 oz) tin kidney beans, drained and rinsed
170 g (6 oz) packet corn chips
½ cup (65 g) grated mozzarella cheese
⅓ cup (85 g) sour cream
½ tomato, finely chopped
¼ red onion, finely diced

1. Preheat the oven to 180°C (350°F) fan-forced.
2. Mash the avocado, garlic, garlic salt and lemon juice in a small bowl. Mix well and set aside.
3. In a small saucepan, heat the leftover bolognese and add the kidney beans. Cook for 5 minutes or until the bolognese sauce has reduced and thickened.
4. On a large baking sheet, or in two separate oven-safe bowls or plates, layer corn chips with the bolognese and then the mozzarella. Bake for 3–5 minutes or until the cheese is melted.
5. Remove from the oven and top with the reserved guacamole and the sour cream, tomato and red onion.

Leah's notes Adding the kidney beans helps to bulk out the bolognese sauce so it goes further. Black beans can also work with this recipe.

Loaded sweet potato

SERVES 1 **PREP TIME** 10 minutes **COOK TIME** 50 minutes

1 medium sweet potato
Olive oil, for coating
2 tablespoons tinned corn kernels
3 cherry tomatoes
½ Lebanese (short) cucumber, diced
¼ red onion, finely diced
Juice of ½ lemon
2 ladles of bolognese sauce (see page 143)
1 small handful melting cheese
2 tablespoons sour cream
Fresh coriander (cilantro), to garnish

1. Preheat the oven to 200°C (400°F) fan-forced. Line a baking tray with baking paper.
2. Coat the sweet potato with olive oil, salt and freshly ground black pepper. Place the sweet potato on the tray and bake for 50 minutes, or until you can pierce it with a knife.
3. Meanwhile, make the salsa. In a small bowl, add the corn kernels, cherry tomatoes, cucumber, red onion and lemon juice. Season with salt and pepper and toss to combine.
4. Remove the sweet potato and slice it in half. Season with salt and pepper. Top with the bolognese sauce and a sprinkle of cheese. Return to the oven and bake until the cheese is melted.
5. Top with salsa and a dollop of sour cream, and sprinkle with coriander to garnish.

Lamb and vegetable roast

p 150

Roast lamb and couscous salad

This easy salad comes together in no time with couscous, that handy pantry staple

p 150

Lamb salad wrap

Crunchy veg, smooth hummus and tasty lamb, all wrapped up

p 151

Quick lamb yiros

Just freshly toast a pita and pile on your toppings for a quick meal

Transform roast lamb leftovers into some stellar lunches: a couscous salad, an easy wrap and the quickest ever Greek yiros.

MAIN RECIPE

Lamb and vegetable roast

SERVES 6

PREP TIME 15 minutes

COOK TIME 6–7 hours

Roasts have been a favourite family dinner in my house from when I was young. This classic version with vegetables also creates an easy gravy in the bottom of the dish.

- 2.5 kg (5 lb 8 oz) bone-in leg of lamb
- 5–6 garlic cloves, thinly sliced
- 4 large rosemary sprigs, leaves picked
- Generous sprinkle of dried oregano
- Juice and zest of 1 lemon (squeezed halves reserved)
- Olive oil, for drizzling
- 3 white potatoes, halved
- 2 carrots, peeled and sliced
- 2 large brown onions, cut into wedges
- 2 cups (500 ml) chicken or beef stock
- 2 tablespoons green peppercorns

1. Preheat the oven to 150°C (300°F) fan-forced.
2. Remove any excess fat from the lamb and use a small knife to pierce small, deep slits all over.
3. In each of the slits, add a few slices of garlic and some fresh rosemary leaves, so the lamb looks colourful.
4. Combine a generous sprinkle of salt, freshly ground black pepper and dried oregano in a bowl. Add the lemon juice and zest with a drizzle of olive oil. Mix to combine and spread over the lamb to completely cover.
5. In the bottom of a deep baking dish, place the potato, carrot, onion and any leftover pieces of rosemary and garlic. Add the lemon halves and season the mixture with salt, pepper, olive oil and oregano.
6. Place the lamb on top and fill the bottom of the tray with the stock. Sprinkle with the green peppercorns. Cover with foil.
7. Cook in the oven for 6–7 hours or until tender.
8. Remove from the oven and allow to rest for at least 15 minutes. Slice the lamb and serve with the vegetables.

Leah's notes Use the juices at the bottom of the roasting pan to make a really delicious gravy. Strain out the peppercorns, add a little cornflour mixed with water and simmer to help thicken it to a gravy consistency.

Roast lamb and couscous salad

SERVES 1 **PREP TIME** 5 minutes **COOK TIME** 10 minutes

¼ cup (50 g) couscous
1 teaspoon (5 g) butter
1 small cucumber, halved and sliced
½ small red onion, thinly sliced
5 pitted Sicilian olives, halved
½ red capsicum (pepper), thinly sliced
5 cherry tomatoes, halved
Olive oil, for drizzling
1 teaspoon white vinegar
½ cup (75 g) shredded leftover roast lamb (see page 149)
2–3 tablespoons tzatziki

1. Prepare the couscous according to the packet instructions, mixing in the butter with the water.
2. Combine the cucumber, red onion, olives, capsicum, cherry tomatoes and cooked couscous in a bowl. Drizzle with a small splash of olive oil and the vinegar. Season with salt and toss to combine.
3. Top with the leftover lamb and a big dollop of tzatziki.

Lamb salad wrap

SERVES 1 **PREP TIME** 5 minutes **COOK TIME** 2 minutes

1 teaspoon za'atar
1 tablespoon olive oil
1 large Lebanese wrap
3 tablespoons hummus
½ cup (75 g) shredded leftover roast lamb (see page 149)
½ cucumber, thinly sliced
3 cherry tomatoes, quartered
1 small handful baby rocket (arugula)
1 tablespoon pickled onions
1 tablespoon toum or tzatziki

1. Combine the za'atar and olive oil in a small bowl. Brush the mixture over both sides of the wrap.
2. Heat a large frying pan over medium heat and toast the wrap for 1 minute on each side or until lightly golden.
3. Smear the hummus on one side and top with the lamb, cucumber, tomatoes, rocket and pickled onions. Drizzle with toum or tzatziki and wrap to enclose.

Quick lamb yiros

SERVES 1 **PREP TIME** 5 minutes **COOK TIME** 2 minutes

1 pita bread
Olive oil spray
1 teaspoon Greek seasoning
3 tablespoons tzatziki
½ cup (75 g) shredded leftover roast lamb (see page 149)
½ small tomato, sliced
¼ cup shredded iceberg lettuce

1. Spray the pita with olive oil on both sides and sprinkle with Greek seasoning.
2. Heat a large frying pan over medium heat and toast the pita for 1 minute on each side or until lightly golden.
3. Spread tzatziki over the wrap. Top with lamb, tomato and lettuce. Roll up to enclose and wrap with foil or baking paper to ensure nothing drips out.

Leah's notes All these recipes work with cold lamb, or you can reheat shredded lamb in a frying pan with a little oil.

Chicken dumplings

p 156

Curried dumpling bake

Try this laksa-inspired bake with Chinese greens

p 156

Dumpling noodle soup

This warming, flavourful broth is so easy and will hit the spot

p 157

Fried dumplings with Asian slaw

This simple slaw with its sweet-salty dressing is perfect with fried dumplings

So many options to use up extra dumplings – try a clever curried dumpling bake, a comforting soup or an Asian-inspired salad.

MAIN RECIPE

Chicken dumplings

SERVES 4 people
(Makes about 60 dumplings)

PREP TIME 30 minutes

COOK TIME 15 minutes

These chicken dumplings are seriously so good – we love these served with some chilli oil and fried rice. They are great to make in big batches for the freezer. You can easily double or triple this recipe to make even more.

500 g (1 lb 2 oz) chicken mince
1 tablespoon soy sauce
1 tablespoon oyster sauce
1 teaspoon white pepper
1 teaspoon chicken bouillon powder
1 tablespoon finely grated ginger
2 garlic cloves, finely grated
1 tablespoon finely grated lemongrass (white part only)
¼ cup (15 g) finely chopped wombok (Chinese cabbage)
1 small carrot, finely grated
3 tablespoons finely chopped chives
60 wonton or dumpling wrappers
Chilli dumpling sauce, to serve

1. Combine the chicken mince, soy sauce, oyster sauce, white pepper and bouillon powder in a large bowl. Add the ginger, garlic, lemongrass, wombok, carrot and chives and mix well.
2. Working one at a time, lay a wonton wrapper down and fill a small bowl with water. Dip your finger into the water and wet around the edges of the wonton wrapper.
3. Add a teaspoon of filling to the middle of the wrapper and fold into the desired dumpling shape, pressing the edges gently to seal. Repeat with the remaining wrappers and filling.
4. To cook, bring a large pot of water to the boil. Gently lower the dumplings into the pot.
5. When the dumplings float, they are cooked (check by spooning one out and cutting it open). Drain well and serve immediately with a chilli dumpling sauce.

Storing instructions Place uncooked dumplings on a lined baking tray, making sure they don't touch. Allow to freeze completely before transferring to a freezer bag or airtight container. To cook, boil or steam from frozen.

Leah's notes Make sure to chop the veggies super small so the filling stays together easily.

Curried dumpling bake

SERVES 4 **PREP TIME** 10 minutes **COOK TIME** 20 minutes

2–3 tablespoons laksa paste
400 ml (14 fl oz) tin coconut milk
2 cups (500 ml) chicken stock
1 tablespoon fish sauce
Juice of 1 lime
2 bok choy, cut in half
1 bunch Chinese broccoli, cut into bite-sized pieces
5–6 button mushrooms, sliced
20 frozen chicken dumplings (see page 155)

1. Preheat the oven to 180°C (350°F) fan-forced.
2. Add the laksa paste, coconut milk and chicken stock to a deep baking dish, and use a fork or mini whisk to mix together well and break up any chunks.
3. Add the fish sauce, lime juice, bok choy, Chinese broccoli and mushrooms to the dish and mix to combine. Place the dumplings on top and push them in deep enough so they're almost submerged.
4. Bake for 20 minutes or until the dumplings are cooked through and tender.

Dumpling noodle soup

SERVES 2 **PREP TIME** 10 minutes **COOK TIME** 25 minutes

½ teaspoon olive oil
2 garlic cloves, crushed
1 tablespoon grated ginger
¼ long red chilli, thinly sliced
1 spring onion (scallion), thinly sliced
4 cups (1 litre) salt-reduced beef stock
2 teaspoons soy sauce
1 teaspoon fish sauce
Juice of ½ lime
125 g (4½ oz) rice noodles, cooked
2 button mushrooms, sliced
½ bunch broccolini, roughly chopped
8 frozen chicken dumplings (see page 155)

1. Heat the olive oil in a small saucepan over low heat. Add the garlic, ginger, chilli and spring onion and cook for 2–3 minutes.
2. Add the stock, soy sauce, fish sauce and lime juice and bring to a low simmer.
3. In a separate bowl, soak the rice noodles to help them cook evenly.
4. Add the mushrooms and broccolini to the pan and cook for 3–5 minutes or until softened. Drain the noodles, then add to the soup and cook for 2 minutes or until softened.
5. Meanwhile, in another saucepan, cook the dumplings in plenty of boiling water until they rise to the top and are cooked.
6. Divide the noodle soup between bowls and top with the dumplings.

Fried dumplings with Asian slaw

SERVES 1 **PREP TIME** 10 minutes **COOK TIME** 15 minutes

2 tablespoons olive oil
5 frozen chicken dumplings (see page 155)
Chilli sauce, to serve (optional)

DRESSING

1 teaspoon toasted sesame seeds
2 tablespoons white wine vinegar
1 tablespoon brown sugar
1 tablespoon soy sauce
1 tablespoon sesame oil
2 tablespoons olive oil

SLAW

¼ red cabbage, shredded
½ carrot, julienned
1 spring onion (scallion), thinly sliced
Small sprinkle of coriander (cilantro) leaves, finely chopped
Small sprinkle of fresh mint, torn

1. Heat the olive oil in a small frying pan. Pan-fry the dumplings for 1–2 minutes or until the bottoms are golden.
2. Add ¼–½ cup water to the pan and cover with a lid. Cook for 5–7 minutes or until the water evaporates. Remove the lid and fry for a few minutes until the dumplings crisp up again.
3. Meanwhile, make the dressing by putting all the ingredients in a jar and shaking to combine.
4. Make the slaw by combining all the ingredients in a bowl. Drizzle the dressing over the slaw and toss to combine. Transfer to a serving bowl.
5. Add the dumplings to the slaw and top with a chilli sauce of your choice (if using).

CHAPTER 4

TAKE ME TO WORK

Your go-to chapter for easy, delicious meals that are perfect to prep ahead and take to work. I know how easy it is to buy lunch out every day, but the price is eye-watering! These recipes are quick to throw together, hold up well in the fridge or lunchbox, and actually taste good when reheated (or even eaten cold).

Chicken meatball bowl with sesame dressing

SERVES 4

PREP TIME 15 minutes (plus 1 hour chilling)

COOK TIME 10 minutes

Meatballs are such a winner. I love doubling this recipe and making a big batch for the freezer. The dressing adds beautiful flavour while keeping the meatballs juicy.

500 g (1 lb 2 oz) chicken mince
¼ cup (30 g) breadcrumbs (add more if mixture is too wet)
2 spring onions (scallions), thinly sliced
1 tablespoon coriander (cilantro), finely chopped
1 tablespoon grated ginger
2 garlic cloves, crushed
1 teaspoon ground turmeric
1 teaspoon sesame oil
1 tablespoon olive oil
Steamed rice, to serve
Cucumber and carrot ribbons, to serve

SESAME DRESSING

2 tablespoons olive oil
¼ cup (60 ml) rice wine vinegar
2 teaspoons honey
2 tablespoons sesame oil
1 tablespoon toasted sesame seeds, plus extra to serve
2 tablespoons soy sauce

1. In a large bowl, combine the chicken mince, breadcrumbs, spring onions, coriander, ginger, garlic, turmeric and sesame oil, season with salt and freshly ground black pepper, and mix to combine.
2. Chill the mixture in the fridge for an hour before forming into meatballs.
3. Roll 1–2 tablespoons of mixture to form a meatball and transfer to a lined tray. Repeat with the remaining mixture.
4. Heat the olive oil in a large frying pan over medium-high heat. Working in batches if necessary, cook the meatballs, turning frequently, for 4-5 minutes or until golden brown and cooked through.
5. To make the sesame dressing, combine all the ingredients in a small jar. Tighten the lid and shake well to combine.
6. Divide the rice between bowls and top with meatballs and cucumber and carrot ribbons. Drizzle with dressing and sprinkle with extra toasted sesame seeds to serve.

Leah's notes Swap out the chicken mince for pork if you prefer.

Chicken Caesar salad

SERVES 4

PREP TIME 20 minutes

COOK TIME 10 minutes

The whole family loves this salad – the homemade croutons are super easy to make and a great way to use up some bread that isn't the freshest.

2 heads baby cos lettuce
8 chicken tenderloins
1 teaspoon each salt and freshly ground black pepper
1 teaspoon dried oregano
1 tablespoon olive oil
200 g (7 oz) shortcut bacon
¾ cup (180 g) Caesar salad dressing (see below for my DIY version, or you can use a store-bought one)
4 hard-boiled eggs, halved
100 g (3½ oz) grated parmesan

OPTIONAL DIY CAESAR DRESSING

½ cup (120 g) mayonnaise
1 garlic clove, crushed
1 teaspoon dijon mustard
¼ cup (25 g) grated parmesan cheese
1 tablespoon lemon juice
1 teaspoon Worcestershire sauce
1 anchovy fillet (optional), finely chopped

GARLIC CROUTONS

4 slices crusty sourdough
1 tablespoon olive oil
½ teaspoon garlic powder
½ teaspoon each salt and freshly ground black pepper

1. For the DIY Caesar dressing (optional), combine all the ingredients in a large bowl. Whisk until smooth and creamy. Season with salt and freshly ground black pepper to taste, then set aside.
2. Wash and drain the baby cos lettuce thoroughly. Chop into large, bite-sized pieces and set aside.
3. To make the garlic croutons, remove the crusts from the bread and cut into bite-sized cubes. Place the bread in a bowl and toss with the olive oil, garlic powder, salt and pepper to coat.
4. Heat a non-stick frying pan over medium-low heat and add the bread cubes. Cook, stirring regularly, until golden brown and crunchy. Transfer to a bowl and set aside.
5. In a medium bowl, toss the chicken with the salt, pepper and oregano. Heat the olive oil in a non-stick frying pan over high heat. Cook the chicken for 3–4 minutes each side or until golden and cooked through. Remove from the pan and allow to cool, then slice into thin strips.
6. Dice the bacon into small pieces and cook in the same pan over medium heat until crisp and lightly browned. Transfer to a paper towel to drain.
7. Add the chopped lettuce, sliced chicken and crispy bacon to the dressing. Toss gently until everything is evenly coated.
8. Divide the salad between four bowls or arrange on a large platter. Top with the garlic croutons, boiled egg halves and a generous sprinkle of grated parmesan.

Leah's notes Save on washing up by using the same frying pan to fry your croutons, then the chicken and lastly the bacon.

Mexican shredded chicken bowls

SERVES 4
PREP TIME 20 minutes
COOK TIME 15 minutes

This recipe comes together so easily, and it's a great one to use up any leftover salad ingredients. The shredded chicken is perfect for meal prep!

800 g (1 lb 12 oz) boneless, skinless chicken thighs
2 medium tomatoes, diced
2 tablespoons chopped coriander (cilantro) leaves, plus extra to serve
½ small red onion, finely diced
420 g (15 oz) tin corn kernels, drained and rinsed
1 tablespoon olive oil
2 cups (370 g) cooked rice (white or brown)
1 large avocado, diced
Sour cream and lime wedges, to serve

MEXICAN MARINADE
2 teaspoons smoked paprika
2 teaspoons ground coriander
2 teaspoons ground cumin
2 teaspoons garlic powder
1 teaspoon each salt and freshly ground black pepper
2 tablespoons olive oil
Juice of 2 limes

1. Make the Mexican marinade by combining all the ingredients in a large bowl.
2. Add the chicken thighs to the marinade and toss to coat evenly. If time allows, marinate the chicken for 20 minutes to develop the flavours.
3. Heat a large non-stick frying pan over high heat and cook the chicken for 5 minutes each side or until browned. Reduce the heat to low, cover with a lid and cook for a further 5 minutes or until the chicken is cooked through.
4. Remove the lid and set the pan aside to let the chicken rest for 5 minutes. Use two forks to shred the chicken into small pieces, mixing it with all the delicious pan juices.
5. Make a tomato salsa by combining the tomato, coriander, red onion, corn and olive oil in a bowl. Season with salt and freshly ground black pepper.
6. Divide the cooked rice between four bowls. Top with shredded chicken, tomato salsa and avocado.
7. Garnish with a dollop of sour cream, some lime wedges and a sprinkle of fresh coriander.

Leah's notes You can use chicken breast instead of chicken thighs here, but just reduce the cooking time to avoid drying the chicken out. If possible, marinate the chicken overnight for an even deeper flavour.

Chicken and chickpea curry

SERVES 4

PREP TIME 10 minutes

COOK TIME 20 minutes

This curry is an amazing way to cook chickpeas; the sauce has a beautiful spice and creaminess to it. I am one of those people who love fresh coriander, so you best believe I will be adding a big handful to mine every time – yum!

2 tablespoons olive oil
1 brown onion, thinly sliced
3 garlic cloves, crushed
2 cm (¾ in) knob of ginger, grated
3 teaspoons ground cumin
3 teaspoons ground turmeric
3 teaspoons garam masala
1 teaspoon ground cardamom
400 g (14 oz) tin crushed tomatoes
2 cups (500 ml) chicken stock
400 ml (14 fl oz) tin coconut cream
420 g (14 oz) tinned chickpeas, drained and rinsed
400 g (14 oz) peeled and diced potato
2 large boneless, skinless chicken breasts, sliced into small strips
Steamed basmati rice, to serve
Coriander (cilantro) sprigs, to garnish

1. Heat the oil in a large, heavy-based saucepan and cook the onion, garlic and ginger over low heat for 3 minutes or until softened.
2. Stir in the cumin, turmeric, garam masala and cardamom and cook for 2 minutes or until fragrant.
3. Add the crushed tomatoes and chicken stock and simmer for 5 minutes. Remove from the stove and purée using a stick blender until smooth.
4. Return the pan to the stove over medium heat and add the coconut cream, chickpeas, potato and chicken.
5. Simmer for 10 minutes or until the potato and chicken are cooked through. Season to taste. Serve with steamed rice and fresh coriander sprigs.

Leah's notes Potato can be swapped out for sweet potato or carrot for added sweetness.

Thai beef salad

SERVES 4

PREP TIME 20 minutes

COOK TIME 10 minutes

This salad is an amazing take-to-work lunch, just keep your beef, salad mix and dressing in separate containers and combine just before you're ready to eat.

500 g (1 lb 2 oz) beef steak, at room temperature
2 tablespoons sesame oil
½ teaspoon each salt and freshly ground black pepper
1 cup (115 g) bean sprouts
1 medium carrot, grated
2 Lebanese (short) cucumbers, halved lengthways and sliced
1 red capsicum (pepper), sliced into thin strips
1 small red onion, thinly sliced
1 handful mint leaves, torn
1 small handful Thai basil leaves, torn
1 small handful coriander (cilantro) leaves, torn
¼ cup (40 g) crushed roasted peanuts
Extra herbs and lime wedges, to garnish

THAI SALAD DRESSING

2 garlic cloves, crushed
½ teaspoon chilli paste
1 small handful coriander (cilantro) leaves and stalks, finely chopped
2 tablespoons white (granulated) sugar
½ cup (125 ml) lime juice
¼ cup (60 ml) rice bran oil
2 tablespoons fish sauce

1. To make the dressing, put all the ingredients in a glass jar with a secure lid. Shake to combine and set aside.
2. Drizzle the beef with the sesame oil and season with the salt and pepper. Heat a medium frying pan over high heat until very hot. Sear the beef for 2–3 minutes each side for medium-rare or until cooked to your liking. Transfer to a board to rest for 5 minutes, then thinly slice against the grain.
3. In a large bowl, combine the bean sprouts, carrot, cucumber, capsicum, onion, mint, Thai basil, coriander and peanuts. Add the cooled sliced beef and dressing. Gently toss to combine all the flavours.
4. Divide the salad between four bowls and top with extra herbs and lime wedges. Serve immediately.

Leah's notes Any good-quality beef steak suitable for fast cooking works well here – think sirloin, fillet, porterhouse, flank or rump. Cook the beef to your liking, but I recommend medium-rare for a juicy and tender result.

Spicy chorizo soup

SERVES 6
PREP TIME 10 minutes
COOK TIME 30 minutes

This is such a good winter warmer. It's hearty and great for getting a bunch of vegetables into you without feeling like you're doing it – sneak it in for the win!

2 × 125 g (4½ oz) spicy chorizo sausages, sliced into half-moons
1 tablespoon olive oil
4 garlic cloves, crushed
4 cm (1½ in) knob of ginger, grated
2 spring onions (scallions), thinly sliced
1 large leek, thinly sliced
1 large carrot, thinly sliced into half-moons
2 zucchini (courgette), thinly sliced into half-moons
3 large celery stalks, thinly sliced
8 cups (2 litres) beef stock
½ × 250 g (9 oz) punnet cherry tomatoes, halved
400 g (14 oz) tin kidney beans, drained and rinsed
2 handfuls kale, shredded
2 handfuls baby spinach

1. Heat a large, heavy-based saucepan over high heat and cook the chorizo until lightly browned. No need for oil here as the chorizo will release its fat as it cooks. Transfer chorizo to a plate.
2. Heat the olive oil in the pan and cook the garlic, ginger and spring onion until lightly softened. Add the leek, carrot, zucchini and celery and cook until they begin to soften.
3. Add the beef stock and cook for 10 minutes. Add the tomatoes, kidney beans and chorizo and cook for a further 10 minutes.
4. Lastly, add kale and baby spinach and cook for 2–3 minutes or until wilted. Divide into bowls to serve.

Leah's notes Spicy chorizo is an easy way to add a heap of flavour to this dish, but it will be just as tasty with mild chorizo if you prefer less heat.

Lamb yiros bowl with turmeric rice

SERVES 4

PREP TIME 15 minutes

COOK TIME 25 minutes

These yiros bowls are perfect when you need a quick and tasty dinner. Using mince speeds up the cooking without losing any flavour – yum!

2 tablespoons olive oil, plus extra for dressing
500 g (1 lb 2 oz) lamb mince
2 tablespoons Greek seasoning or dried oregano
10 cherry tomatoes, sliced
1 small Lebanese (short) cucumber, sliced into rounds
1 small red capsicum (pepper), thinly sliced
½ red onion, thinly sliced
5–8 pitted kalamata olives
¼ cup (35 g) crumbled feta cheese
Juice of ½ lemon, or to taste
Sprinkle of dried oregano
1 pita bread
Olive oil spray
½ cup (130 g) tzatziki, or more to your liking

TURMERIC RICE

1 cup (200 g) basmati rice
2 cups (500 ml) chicken stock
1 teaspoon ground turmeric

1. Heat the olive oil in a large frying pan over medium-high heat. Cook the lamb mince and Greek seasoning for 5–6 minutes or until browned and cooked through. Set aside.
2. To make the turmeric rice, combine all the ingredients in a medium, heavy-based saucepan. Bring to the boil, reduce the heat to medium–low and simmer, covered, for 15 minutes or until the rice is tender. Remove from the heat and set aside, covered, for a few minutes before fluffing with a fork.
3. In a large bowl, combine the cherry tomatoes, cucumber, capsicum, red onion, olives and feta. Dress with the lemon juice, oregano, a drizzle of olive oil and a pinch of salt. Toss everything together until well mixed.
4. Lightly spray the pita bread with olive oil. Heat the frying pan over medium heat (no need to wash it!) and warm the pita bread on both sides until golden and soft. Cut the pita bread into wedges.
5. Divide the turmeric rice, lamb mince and salad between bowls. Add a side of warm pita bread and top everything with a generous dollop of tzatziki.

Leah's notes Any type of mince would work in this recipe – feel free to switch it up depending on what your family prefers.

Honey-garlic chicken bowls

SERVES 4

PREP TIME 10 minutes

COOK TIME 15 minutes

Super quick and easy, there's no marinating required for this delicious tasty chicken. Definitely a dinnertime favourite.

8 boneless, skinless chicken thighs, cut in half
1 teaspoon each salt and freshly ground black pepper
¼ cup (30 g) cornflour (cornstarch)
2 tablespoons rice bran oil
1 tablespoon minced garlic
½ cup (175 g) honey
½ cup (125 ml) chicken stock
1 tablespoon rice wine vinegar
1 tablespoon light soy sauce
4 cups (740 g) cooked rice
Thinly sliced spring onions (scallions), to serve
Dried chilli flakes, to garnish (optional)

1. Place the chicken in a bowl and season with the salt and pepper. Add the cornflour and toss until evenly coated.
2. Heat the rice bran oil in a large frying pan over high heat. When the oil is hot, cook the chicken for 3–4 minutes each side or until golden brown.
3. Reduce the heat to low and add the garlic. Cook for 1 minute, stirring constantly to avoid burning.
4. Pour in the honey, chicken stock, vinegar and soy sauce. Stir to combine and simmer over medium–low heat for 5–7 minutes, or until the chicken is cooked through and the sauce has thickened slightly.
5. Divide the rice between bowls. Top with the honey-garlic chicken and spoon over any extra sauce. Garnish with spring onions and a sprinkle of chilli flakes (if using).

Leah's notes You can use chicken breast but you'll need to reduce your cooking times to avoid the chicken drying out.

Garlic chorizo pasta

SERVES 4
PREP TIME 10 minutes
COOK TIME 15 minutes

I love pasta with an olive oil base and this is such a tasty recipe to whip up when you don't have a lot of time. We love this as a side dish at a barbecue and it makes great leftovers.

500 g (1 lb 2 oz) fusilli (spiral) pasta
¼ cup (60 ml) olive oil
300 g (10½ oz) mild chorizo, sliced
1 small red onion, thinly sliced
2 garlic cloves, crushed
1 large red capsicum (pepper), cut into strips
100 g (3½ oz) baby spinach leaves
1 cup (155 g) semi-dried tomato strips

1. Cook the pasta according to the packet instructions. Drain and set aside.
2. Heat the olive oil in a large frying pan over medium heat. Add the chorizo and onion and cook gently for 5 minutes or until the onion has softened and the chorizo is slightly crisp.
3. Add the garlic and capsicum and cook for a further 5 minutes, or until the capsicum is tender.
4. Remove the pan from the heat. Add the cooked pasta, baby spinach and semi-dried tomatoes and gently toss to combine.
5. Season generously with freshly ground black pepper and divide between bowls to serve.

Leah's notes Some prawns would also be delicious in this recipe with the chorizo – feel free to jazz it up to suit the flavours you love.

Spiced chicken meatballs and rainbow salad

SERVES 4

PREP TIME 10 minutes

COOK TIME 10 minutes

The colours in this easy meal wow me every time! The mildly spiced meatballs go perfectly with a bright and zesty mayo.

500 g (1 lb 2 oz) chicken mince
1 tablespoon toasted sesame seeds
4 garlic cloves, crushed
2 tablespoons finely grated ginger
1½ tablespoons curry powder
2 spring onions (scallions), finely chopped
1 small handful coriander (cilantro) leaves, finely chopped
1 tablespoon olive oil

ZESTY LIME MAYO

½ cup (120 g) whole-egg mayonnaise
1 garlic clove, crushed
Zest and juice of 1 lime

RAINBOW SALAD

¼ red cabbage, shredded
1 large carrot, grated
Drizzle of olive oil and white wine vinegar, for dressing

1. Combine the chicken mince, sesame seeds, garlic, ginger, curry powder, spring onion and coriander in a large bowl. Season with salt and freshly ground black pepper. Mix well with your hands to combine. Using roughly 1 tablespoon of mixture at a time, roll into meatballs.
2. To make the lime mayo, combine all the ingredients in a small bowl and season to taste.
3. To make the rainbow salad, combine the cabbage and carrot in a large bowl. Drizzle with olive oil and vinegar. Season with salt and toss to combine.
4. Heat the olive oil in a medium non-stick frying pan over medium heat. Cook the meatballs, turning, for 7–8 minutes or until completely cooked through.
5. Top the salad with the meatballs. Drizzle with the zesty lime mayo to serve.

Leah's notes The same flavours also work great with pork mince.

Roast vegetable and bean salad

SERVES 4
PREP TIME 10 minutes
COOK TIME 30 minutes

This roast vegetable salad is perfect for a vegetarian meal, but adding something like chicken schnitzels or a different protein on top is such a good way of pleasing everyone!

1 small eggplant (aubergine), cut into small cubes
120 g (4¼ oz) pumpkin (squash), peeled and cut into small cubes
½ sweet potato, cut into small cubes
1 red capsicum (pepper), cut into small cubes
1 red onion, cut into thin wedges
1 potato, cut into small cubes
2 tablespoons olive oil
1 teaspoon salt
½ teaspoon freshly ground black pepper
1 teaspoon sweet paprika
1 teaspoon garlic powder
400 g (14 oz) tin butter beans, drained and rinsed
2 handfuls baby rocket (arugula)
100 g (3½ oz) feta cheese, crumbled
Balsamic vinegar, to taste

1. Preheat the oven to 200°C (400°F) fan-forced. Line a baking tray with baking paper.
2. Combine the eggplant, pumpkin, sweet potato, capsicum, red onion and potato in a large bowl. Drizzle with the olive oil. Add the salt, pepper, paprika and garlic powder. Toss until evenly coated.
3. Transfer the vegetables to the baking tray and roast for 25–30 minutes or until cooked through (the cook time will depend on the size of your vegetables). In the last 5 minutes, add the butter beans to the tray and toss to combine.
4. Combine the rocket, feta and the vegetable-bean mixture in a large bowl. Season with olive oil, salt and a drizzle of balsamic vinegar to taste. Toss to combine and serve.

Leah's notes Cut your veggies smaller for a quicker cook time.

Grilled chicken and quinoa salad

SERVES 4
PREP TIME 10 minutes
COOK TIME 15 minutes

Quinoa is a fancy-pants grain in my opinion, but it's such a goodie! It's a complete protein and high in fibre, so this is a great option to sneak in extra goodness.

1 cup (200 g) quinoa
500 g (1 lb 2 oz) boneless, skinless chicken breast, sliced into strips
2 tablespoons olive oil, plus extra to drizzle
½ teaspoon salt
½ teaspoon freshly ground black pepper
1 teaspoon dried oregano
Juice of 1 lemon
½ teaspoon paprika
½ teaspoon garlic powder
1 large Lebanese (short) cucumber, sliced into half-moons
12 cherry tomatoes, halved
½ red onion, thinly sliced
100 g (3½ oz) feta cheese, crumbled
12 pitted kalamata olives
Balsamic glaze, to drizzle

1. Cook the quinoa according to the packet instructions and set aside.
2. Combine the chicken with the olive oil, salt, pepper, dried oregano, lemon juice, paprika and garlic powder in a bowl. Mix to coat well.
3. Heat a drizzle of olive oil in a medium non-stick frying pan over medium-high heat and cook the chicken for 5–6 minutes or until cooked through. Transfer to a plate to rest.
4. Meanwhile, add the cooked quinoa, cucumber, cherry tomatoes, red onion, feta cheese and olives to a large bowl. Drizzle with olive oil, season with salt and drizzle with balsamic glaze. Toss to combine.
5. Serve the quinoa salad topped with the chicken.

Leah's notes You can pre-marinate your meat and freeze it. Once defrosted, throw straight into the pan. The flavours will soak into the chicken and be even more delicious!

Curried pumpkin soup

SERVES 4
PREP TIME 10 minutes
COOK TIME 30 minutes

When you're in need of a winter warmer, this is it! It's a little twist on regular pumpkin soup, so it feels extra fancy.

1 tablespoon olive oil
2 tablespoons Thai red curry paste
2 French shallots, roughly chopped
4 garlic cloves
1 kg (2 lb 4 oz) kent pumpkin (squash), peeled and roughly chopped
3 carrots, peeled and roughly chopped
4 cups (1 litre) vegetable stock
2 tablespoons soy sauce
2 tablespoons fish sauce
400 ml (14 fl oz) tin coconut cream

1. Heat a large, heavy-based saucepan with olive oil over medium heat. Cook the curry paste for 1–2 minutes or until fragrant.
2. Add the shallots and garlic and cook for a further 1–2 minutes or until slightly softened.
3. Add the pumpkin and carrot and stir until coated. Add the stock and cook for 25 minutes or until the vegetables are tender.
4. Purée the soup with a stick blender until smooth. Stir in the soy sauce, fish sauce and coconut cream (reserve a little coconut cream to garnish). Divide the soup between bowls, add the reserved coconut cream and swirl to create a gorgeous top.

Leah's notes Make sure you find a mild curry paste, or your soup will be super spicy! If you're wanting to freeze this, divide the soup into single-serve containers and freeze for up to 3 months.

Speedy chicken fried rice

SERVES 4
PREP TIME 10 minutes
COOK TIME 20 minutes

Fried rice, yes please! This recipe is so delicious. If you're not a fan of chilli, use an olive oil for the beginning of the cooking as it can get quite spicy.

2 cups (400 g) basmati rice
2 tablespoons chilli oil plus 1 tablespoon chilli crisp (see page 83)
500 g (1 lb 2 oz) chicken mince
¼ cup (60 ml) soy sauce
¼ cup (60 ml) oyster sauce
2 tablespoons kecap manis
1 tablespoon curry powder
3 garlic cloves, crushed
2 tablespoons grated ginger
2 cups (300 g) frozen vegetables
1 tablespoon sesame oil
2 eggs, whisked

1. Cook the basmati rice according to the packet instructions. Fluff with a fork and set aside.
2. Meanwhile, heat the chilli oil in a large wok over medium heat. Cook the chicken mince, breaking it up into small pieces, for 5–6 minutes or until lightly browned.
3. Mix together the soy sauce, oyster sauce, kecap manis and curry powder in a small bowl and set aside.
4. Add the garlic and ginger to the chicken and stir-fry for 1 minute. Push the mixture to the side and add the vegetables. Stir-fry on high heat for 2–3 minutes or until the vegetables start to soften. Season with salt and freshly ground black pepper.
5. Combine the chicken and vegetable mixture and push to the side of the wok. Pour the sesame oil into the wok. Add the eggs and cook, stirring occasionally, until lightly scrambled, then combine with the chicken and veggie mixture.
6. Add the rice to the wok with the soy sauce mixture. Stir-fry over medium heat until combined.
7. Stir through the 1 tablespoon chilli crisp and serve.

Leah's notes This is a great one to throw a packet of frozen veggies into! You can use whatever veggies you like, but a frozen packet saves so much cutting/cooking time.

GOT TIME? I'VE GOT YOU.

CHAPTER 5

This chapter is for when you've actually got a spare hour (or two!) to cook and you're not rushing out the door or juggling a million things. Whether it's my yiayia's spanakopita, my favourite dumplings or a slow-cooked ragu, these recipes are perfect for weekends, entertaining or just when you feel like trying something a little more fun.

Each one makes four meals plus two portions to keep for later, and the freezing tips mean you can stash the extra away and they'll come to the rescue another night. So, if you've got a bit more time, this chapter is your excuse to put on your favourite playlist and get cooking.

Mushroom and asparagus risotto

SERVES 6

PREP TIME 20 minutes

COOK TIME 30–40 minutes

Risotto is one of those meals that just gets better each day – this is perfect to prep ahead and reheat throughout the week.

¼ cup (60 ml) olive oil
300 g (10½ oz) Swiss brown mushrooms, thinly sliced
300 g (10½ oz) button mushrooms, thinly sliced
200 g (7 oz) portobello mushrooms, thinly sliced
1 bunch (about 150 g/5½ oz) asparagus, chopped
1 brown onion, finely diced
2–3 garlic cloves, crushed
2½ cups (550 g) arborio rice, unwashed
1 tablespoon ground turmeric
1 red chilli, finely chopped (optional)
6–7 cups (1.5–1.75 litres) chicken stock, warmed
⅓ cup (35 g) parmesan cheese, finely grated, plus extra to serve

1. Heat 1 tablespoon of the olive oil in a large heavy-based pan over medium heat. Add all the mushrooms and cook for 8–10 minutes or until golden and the liquid has evaporated. Transfer the mushroom mixture to a plate and set aside.
2. In the same pan, heat another tablespoon of olive oil over medium heat. Cook the asparagus for 2 minutes or until just tender. Transfer to the plate with the mushrooms.
3. Heat the remaining tablespoon of oil in the same pan. Add the onion, garlic and the rice and cook, stirring, for a few minutes. Add the turmeric and chilli (if using) and stir to combine.
4. Add the hot stock, one ladleful at a time, stirring regularly and waiting for the stock to be absorbed before adding another ladleful. Halfway through adding the stock, stir in the asparagus and mushroom mixture.
5. Continue adding stock until absorbed and the rice is cooked to your liking.
6. Add the parmesan cheese and stir well to combine. Serve sprinkled with extra parmesan.

Storing instructions Allow to cool completely then freeze in an airtight container for up to one month.

Leah's notes Adding the stock one ladle at a time does take longer, but it's a key part of what makes this so creamy and delicious.

Spanakopita

SERVES 6

PREP TIME 20 minutes (plus cooling)

COOK TIME 40–50 minutes

This spanakopita is so delicious fresh out of the oven when the pastry is crispy and golden. We love this served with a fresh salad on the side.

- 1 large bunch English spinach, coarsely chopped
- 2 spring onions (scallions), finely chopped
- 1 leek, finely chopped
- 2 garlic cloves, crushed
- 3 eggs, whisked
- 2 tablespoons chopped dill
- 200 g (7 oz) feta, crumbled
- 200 g (7 oz) ricotta, crumbled
- 1 teaspoon salt, or to taste
- 1 tablespoon freshly ground black pepper, or to taste
- 3 tablespoons (60 g) butter, melted
- 10 sheets filo pastry
- 2 tablespoons sesame seeds

1. Preheat the oven to 180°C (350°F) fan-forced.
2. Heat a medium frying pan over medium heat. Cook the spinach, spring onion, leek and garlic for 5 minutes or until the spinach is wilted and the leek translucent.
3. Transfer to a large mixing bowl and set aside to cool.
4. Once cooled, gently squeeze out the excess liquid from the greens over the sink, then place back in the bowl. Add the eggs, dill, feta, ricotta, salt and pepper to the greens. Mix well until combined.
5. Brush the bottom of a large baking dish with some melted butter. Place a sheet of filo on the bottom of the dish and brush with butter again. Repeat this four times, brushing with butter after each layer and ensuring the filo is well coated.
6. Add all the cooled spanakopita mixture on top of the filo pastry and gently spread it out.
7. Layer another five filo sheets on top, brushing butter in between each layer and making sure the pastry is well coated. Scrunch the filo edges down around the sides of the dish.
8. Sprinkle sesame seeds over the top of the final layer of pastry.
9. Bake for 30–45 minutes (checking after 30 minutes to ensure it doesn't burn) or until golden brown.

Storing instructions Allow to cool completely, cut into pieces and freeze in an airtight container for up to 2 months. This is best reheated in the oven or air fryer; the microwave won't work here.

Leah's notes Allowing the mixture to cool before adding it to the filo ensures the pastry doesn't fall apart when assembling.

Roast vegetable soup

SERVES 6
PREP TIME 20 minutes
COOK TIME 35 minutes

This soup is perfect to freeze in individual portions. Simply heat up for a quick and delicious lunch or dinner.

1 large sweet potato, peeled and chopped
3 white potatoes, peeled and chopped
300 g (10½ oz) butternut pumpkin (squash), peeled and chopped
1 leek, thickly sliced
2 brown onions, roughly chopped
2 medium carrots, roughly chopped
1 fennel bulb, thickly sliced
1 tablespoon dried rosemary
1 tablespoon thyme leaves
¼ cup (60 ml) olive oil
1 garlic bulb
6 cups (1.5 litres) chicken or vegetable stock
200 ml (7 fl oz) coconut milk
Chopped coriander (cilantro) or flat-leaf parsley, to serve

1. Preheat the oven to 200°C (400°F) fan-forced. Line a baking tray with baking paper.
2. Combine the sweet potato, potato, pumpkin, leek, onion, carrot and fennel on the baking tray. Sprinkle with rosemary and thyme and season with salt and freshly ground black pepper. Drizzle with 2 tablespoons of the olive oil and toss to combine. Spread out in an even layer.
3. Place the garlic bulb on a piece of foil, drizzle with the remaining tablespoon of olive oil and wrap to enclose tightly. Nestle the garlic in the veggies on the baking tray.
4. Roast the veggies for around 30 minutes or until the vegetables are tender enough to run a fork through.
5. Set the tray aside to cool slightly.
6. Once cool enough to handle, remove the garlic from the foil and squeeze the cloves out into a blender, ensuring no skin is included. Transfer the roasted vegetables to the blender along with half the stock.
7. Start blending, gradually adding the remaining stock, until the soup reaches your desired consistency.
8. Transfer the soup to a stockpot and slowly bring it to a simmer over medium heat. Once simmering, reduce the heat to low and stir in the coconut milk.
9. Divide between bowls and sprinkle with coriander or parsley to serve.

Storing instructions Freeze in an airtight container for up to 3 months. I always freeze in single serves so it's easy to grab and go.

Leah's notes Taking the time to roast the vegetables first adds a great depth of flavour to this soup.

Roast lamb yiros

SERVES 6

PREP TIME 20 minutes

COOK TIME 3.5 hours

Yiros for dinner is a family favourite, they pack so much flavour and the meat is great to make ahead of time, plus... we're Greek! No wonder it's a weekly meal here.

1.5 kg (3 lb 5 oz) leg of lamb
7–8 garlic cloves, thinly sliced
2 tablespoons olive oil
1 tablespoon dried oregano
1 tablespoon dried thyme
1 tablespoon dried rosemary
2 tablespoons dijon mustard
2 tablespoons smoked paprika
1 brown onion, grated
Juice of ½ lemon
1 tablespoon salt, or to taste
1 tablespoon freshly ground black pepper
1 garlic bulb, sliced in half horizontally
2 cups (500 ml) beef stock
6 pita breads
200 g (7 oz) tzatziki
Shredded iceberg lettuce and tomato slices, to serve

1. Preheat the oven to 180°C (350°F) fan-forced.
2. Using a small knife, carefully cut slits into the lamb and insert sliced garlic cloves in the slits.
3. In a medium bowl, combine the oil with the oregano, thyme, rosemary, mustard, paprika, grated onion, lemon juice, salt and pepper. Mix really well to form a paste.
4. Using your hands, rub the paste all over the lamb until the surface is completely covered.
5. Place the lamb in a large roasting dish with the garlic bulb and beef stock. Roast for 3 hours or until cooked and falling apart when separated with a fork.
6. Set aside to rest for 15 minutes to allow the lamb to soak up all the juices.
7. Once rested, slice the lamb and season with salt or pepper.
8. Lightly spray each pita with oil. Heat a small frying pan over medium heat and cook the pita breads for 1–2 minutes each side or until warmed through.
9. Smear each pita with tzatziki, then top with lamb, lettuce and tomato. Roll up and enjoy.

Storing instructions The cooked meat mixture can be stored in the freezer for up to 3 months.

Leah's notes Feel free to add another sauce, such as sriracha, to spice things up.

Prawn dumplings

SERVES 6 (Makes about 60 dumplings)

PREP TIME 30 minutes

COOK TIME 5 minutes

Prawn dumplings have my whole heart... My mum makes huge batches of these and pops them in my freezer whenever she's at my house. It's like an unspoken love language.

- 500 g (1 lb 2 oz) raw banana prawns, peeled and deveined
- 1 tablespoon soy sauce
- 1 teaspoon white pepper
- 1 tablespoon grated ginger
- 3 garlic cloves, finely grated
- ¼ cup (10 g) wombok (Chinese cabbage), finely chopped
- 4 Swiss brown mushrooms, finely diced
- 1 small handful coriander (cilantro) leaves, finely chopped
- 1 spring onion (scallion), finely chopped, plus extra to serve
- 60 wonton or dumpling wrappers
- Chilli dumpling sauce, to serve

1. Add the prawns to a blender and blend until small chunks form (not a paste!). Transfer the prawns to a bowl with the soy sauce, white pepper, ginger, garlic, wombok, mushrooms, coriander and spring onion. Mix well to combine. Line a baking tray with baking paper.
2. Lay the wonton wrappers down and fill a small bowl with water. Dip your finger into the water and wet around the edges of a wonton wrapper.
3. Add a teaspoon of filling to the middle of the wrapper and fold into the desired dumpling shape, pressing gently to seal the edges. Place on the lined tray and repeat.
4. To cook, bring a large pot of water to the boil.
5. Gently lower the dumplings into the pot and cook for 5 minutes or until they float to the top. Drain well when removing. Serve immediately with a chilli dumpling sauce and sprinkled with spring onion.

Storing instructions Place uncooked dumplings on a lined baking tray, making sure they don't touch. Allow to freeze completely before transferring into a freezer bag or airtight container. To cook, boil or steam from frozen.

Leah's notes These are great to make in big batches for the freezer. You can easily double or triple this recipe to make even more.

Spinach, ricotta and chicken lasagne

SERVES 6
PREP TIME 30 minutes
COOK TIME 1 hour

Lasagne is one of those dishes that everyone loves. This is great to make when feeding a lot of people. It reheats so well too – perfect for leftovers.

2 tablespoons olive oil
1 brown onion, finely diced
2 garlic cloves, crushed
500 g (1 lb 2 oz) English spinach, washed and roughly chopped
500 g (1 lb 2 oz) ricotta cheese
1 egg
2 cups (300 g) shredded barbecue chicken
1 tablespoon dijon mustard
1 tablespoon (20 g) melted butter
4 cups (1 kg) napoletana sauce (store-bought or made from scratch, see page 103)
8-12 lasagne sheets
1 cup (100 g) grated parmesan cheese
1½ cups (190 g) grated mozzarella cheese

1. Preheat the oven to 180°C (350°F) fan-forced.
2. Heat the oil in a large frying pan over medium-high heat. Cook the onion, stirring, for 6–8 minutes or until translucent.
3. Add the garlic and cook for a further 2 minutes or until golden in colour and fragrant, being careful not to burn it. Transfer to a large bowl and set aside to cool slightly.
4. Add the spinach, ricotta, egg, chicken and mustard to the onion mixture. Stir well to combine thoroughly.
5. Season with a good pinch of salt and freshly ground pepper and mix to combine.
6. Brush the bottom of a large baking dish with the melted butter. Add a ladle of napoletana sauce, spreading it to cover the bottom of the dish.
7. Follow this with a layer of the spinach and ricotta mixture, then a lasagne sheet. Add another ladle of napoletana sauce and a handful of parmesan cheese.
8. Continue to alternate layers of napoletana sauce, spinach and ricotta mixture, parmesan and lasagne until all used up. Finish with the mozzarella cheese.
9. Cover with foil and bake for 30 minutes. Uncover then cook for a further 10–15 minutes or until the cheese is melted and golden on top. Leave to stand for 10 minutes before slicing so it is able to set.

Storing instructions Slice into individual portions and place in airtight containers for up to 3 months in the freezer.

Leah's notes Fresh or dried lasagne sheets both work well in this recipe – use whatever you have at home.

Lamb ragu

SERVES 6

PREP TIME 30 minutes

COOK TIME 2.5 hours

This is such a versatile meal to prepare ahead of time. We love this served over pasta, with rice or even in a lasagne. Yum!

1.5 kg (3 lb 5 oz) boneless lamb shoulder roast, cut into bite-sized pieces
1 tablespoon each salt and freshly ground black pepper
2 tablespoons olive oil
2 brown onions, finely chopped
3 garlic cloves, crushed
1 red chilli, finely chopped (optional)
2 tablespoons tomato paste (concentrated purée)
1 large carrot, finely chopped
4 celery stalks, finely chopped
1 teaspoon freshly ground nutmeg
1 teaspoon ground allspice
1 cinnamon stick
2 bay leaves
2 × 400 g (14 oz) tins crushed tomatoes
Steamed rice, torn basil leaves and crusty bread, to serve

1. Preheat the oven to 180°C (350°F) fan-forced.
2. In a large bowl, place the lamb and salt and pepper and toss well to combine.
3. Heat 1 tablespoon of the olive oil in a large ovenproof saucepan over medium-high heat and cook the lamb in batches for 10–15 minutes or until browned all over. Transfer to a plate.
4. In the same pan, heat the remaining tablespoon of oil and cook the onion for 3–4 minutes or until translucent. Stir in the garlic and chilli and cook for a further 2 minutes.
5. Add the tomato paste and cook, stirring, for 2 minutes or until darkened.
6. Stir in the carrot and celery along with the nutmeg, allspice, cinnamon and bay leaves and cook for 5 minutes or until fragrant.
7. Add the crushed tomatoes and return the lamb to the pan. Stir well so the lamb is completely covered.
8. Cover with a lid and bake for 1 hour 30 minutes.
9. Uncover and bake for a further 30 minutes or until the meat is fork-tender and falling apart.
10. Shred the meat into the sauce and mix well, seasoning with salt and pepper to taste.
11. Serve over rice and top with basil leaves. Don't forget crusty bread for soaking up the delicious sauce.

Storing instructions Allow to cool completely. Remove the cinnamon stick and bay leaves, then freeze in an airtight container for up to 3 months.

Leah's notes Using crushed tomatoes is an important step in this recipe – they add the liquid needed to keep the meat juicy.

Vegetable lasagne

SERVES 6
PREP TIME 30 minutes
COOK TIME 1 hour

We love this lasagne. The ribbons of veggies are an easy way to pack extra vegetables into this meal – they layer so well and are great for soaking up that delicious sauce.

2 tablespoons olive oil
1 large brown onion, thinly sliced
2 garlic cloves, crushed
2 large zucchini (courgette), peeled into ribbons
1 large sweet potato, peeled into ribbons
1 eggplant (aubergine), peeled into ribbons
2 red capsicums (peppers), thickly sliced
120 g (4¼ oz) baby spinach leaves
1 tablespoon dried oregano
2 tablespoons smoked paprika
1 tablespoon (20 g) melted butter, for the dish
4 cups (1 kg) napoletana sauce (store-bought or made from scratch, see page 103)
300 g (10½ oz) grated melting cheese, such as mozzarella
8 fresh lasagne sheets (depending on size of dish)
200 g (7 oz) parmesan cheese, grated

1. Preheat the oven to 180°C (350°F) fan-forced.
2. Heat the olive oil in a frying pan over low heat and cook the onion and garlic for 4-5 minutes or until the onion is translucent. Transfer to a large bowl.
3. Add the zucchini, sweet potato and eggplant along with the capsicum and spinach to the onion mixture. Toss well to combine. Add the oregano and paprika and season with salt and freshly ground black pepper. Mix thoroughly.
4. Brush the bottom of a large baking dish with the melted butter. Add a ladle of napoletana sauce, spreading to cover the bottom of the dish.
5. Start layering the vegetable mixture, ensuring that the ribbons of veggies form a single layer. Top with mozzarella cheese, more napoletana sauce and lasagne sheets.
6. Repeat these layers until all of the veggies and lasagne sheets have been used, finishing with a layer of mozzarella. Sprinkle with the parmesan.
7. Cover with foil and bake for 30 minutes. Uncover then cook for a further 10–15 minutes or until the cheese is melted and golden on top.
8. Stand for 10 minutes to allow the lasagne to set before slicing.

Storing instructions Allow to cool, then slice into desired portions. Freeze in an airtight container for up to 3 months.

Leah's notes Use a vegetable peeler to get ribbons of veggies, or a mandoline if you have one.

Curry chicken and corn pie

SERVES 6
PREP TIME 15 minutes
COOK TIME 1 hour

This pie is so creamy and delicious. I love to make this mixture ahead of time to freeze. Then I simply thaw it overnight and top with pastry for a quick and tasty dinner.

1 tablespoon olive oil
1 brown onion, finely diced
4 garlic cloves, crushed
1 leek, thinly sliced
1 teaspoon ground turmeric
1 tablespoon curry powder
½ cup (125 g) sour cream
1 cup (250 ml) chicken stock
420 g (15 oz) tin corn kernels, drained
1 barbecue chicken, meat shredded
2 sheets puff pastry, thawed
1 egg, whisked
1 tablespoon sesame seeds

1. Preheat the oven to 180°C (350°F) fan-forced.
2. Heat the olive oil in a large saucepan over medium heat. Add the onion and cook for 3 minutes or until translucent. Add the garlic and leek and cook for 5 minutes, stirring well to ensure the garlic doesn't burn.
3. Stir in the turmeric and curry powder and cook for 1–2 minutes or until fragrant and combined.
4. Add the sour cream, chicken stock, corn and shredded chicken. Stir well to combine and cook for 10 minutes or until the mixture has slightly thickened. Season to taste with salt and freshly ground black pepper.
5. Fill a large pie dish or individual ramekins with the pie filling and top with puff pastry, trimming the pastry as necessary to fit. Press down around the edges to seal.
6. Brush the pastry with the whisked egg and sprinkle with sesame seeds.
7. Bake for 25–30 minutes or until golden brown on top.

Storing instructions Freeze the cooked and cooled mixture in an airtight container for up to 3 months. Thaw overnight in the fridge and transfer to a baking dish. Top with pastry and bake as directed.

Leah's notes If the pie filling is too thin, make a cornstarch slurry by mixing 1 tablespoon cornflour and 1 tablespoon water in a small bowl. Slowly add the slurry to the chicken mixture, stirring well and cooking for a few minutes until the mixture thickens.

Slow-cooked osso bucco

SERVES 6

PREP TIME 15 minutes

COOK TIME 2.5 hours

This is the ultimate comforting winter meal – we love this with a slice of fresh bread to soak up all that delicious sauce.

1.5 kg (3 lb 5 oz) osso bucco
Zest of 1 lemon
3 thyme sprigs
2 tablespoons plain (all-purpose) flour
¼ cup (60 ml) olive oil
1 large carrot, finely chopped
2 celery stalks, finely chopped
2 garlic cloves, crushed
1 large potato, finely chopped
1 cup (250 ml) dry white wine
2 × 400 g (14 oz) tins crushed tomato
2 cups (500 ml) beef stock
1 bay leaf
Mashed potato, to serve

1. Preheat the oven to 180°C (350°F) fan-forced.
2. Pat the osso bucco dry with paper towel and place it in a large bowl. Add the lemon zest, thyme and flour. Generously season with salt and freshly ground black pepper. Mix thoroughly, making sure all the meat is coated.
3. Heat 1 tablespoon of the olive oil in a large ovenproof saucepan and sear the meat in batches for 3–4 minutes each side or until browned. Transfer to a plate.
4. Add the remaining 2 tablespoons of oil to the pan and cook the carrot, celery, garlic and potato for a few minutes. Stir in the wine, scraping the bottom of the pan to loosen everything. This is key to creating a delicious flavour.
5. Once the wine has evaporated, add the crushed tomatoes, beef stock and bay leaf. Return the meat back to the pan, making sure it is completely covered with the sauce. Taste and season with salt and pepper.
6. Cover with a lid and bake for 2 hours. Uncover for the last 15 minutes to get a deeper colour on the meat.
7. Serve with mashed potato.

Storing instructions Once completely cooled, freeze in an airtight container for up to 3 months.

Leah's notes The white wine is optional in this dish – leave it out if you like.

Beef curry

SERVES 6

PREP TIME 10 minutes

COOK TIME 6.5 hours

Remember going for a walk past your neighbour's house and smelling their delicious meal wafting through the air? Well, this recipe will make YOU the neighbour with the delicious smelling dinner! This beef curry is the best winter recipe – no curry paste needed, just a slow cooker and a few simple spices.

2 tablespoons rice bran oil
1 kg (2 lb 4 oz) diced chuck steak
1 brown onion, sliced
4 large potatoes, peeled and chopped into large pieces
3 teaspoons ground cumin
3 teaspoons ground coriander
1 teaspoon ground turmeric
3 teaspoons garam masala
1 teaspoon dried chilli flakes
3 garlic cloves
2 tablespoons grated ginger
¼ cup (75 g) tomato paste (concentrated purée)
400 ml (14 fl oz) tin coconut cream
2 tablespoons raw sugar
Steamed basmati rice, to serve
Coriander (cilantro) leaves, to garnish

1. Heat the rice bran oil in a large frying pan over high heat. Cook the beef in small batches for 15 minutes or until browned. Transfer directly into a slow cooker.
2. Add all the remaining ingredients to the slow cooker, except the coconut cream and sugar. Stir gently to combine. You want to make sure all of the beef is generously coated in those beautiful spices (add a little more spice if you need!). Cook on low for 6 hours or until the beef is tender.
3. Just before serving, add the coconut cream and sugar and stir until combined.
4. Serve on steamed rice. Garnish with coriander leaves.

Storing instructions Allow to cool completely, then divide into desired portion sizes (I find individual ones the easiest for reheating). These can be frozen for up to 3 months.

Leah's notes If you're short on time you can skip browning the beef and place it straight into the slow cooker; it will still taste delicious.

Butter chicken rice bake

SERVES 6

PREP TIME 10 minutes

COOK TIME 1 hour

This recipe is something I dream about! As soon as it comes to me, it's a necessity for that night AND breakfast the next day (don't knock it until you try it).

600 g (1 lb 5 oz) chicken tenderloins, sliced into bite-sized pieces
170 g (6 oz) plain yoghurt
½ teaspoon salt
½ teaspoon freshly ground black pepper
1 teaspoon garam masala
½ teaspoon chilli powder
½ teaspoon ground cumin
¾ cup (150 g) basmati rice, rinsed
2 cups (500 ml) chicken stock, warmed
Chopped coriander (cilantro), to garnish

BUTTER CHICKEN SAUCE
1 tablespoon (20 g) butter
1 small brown onion, finely diced
3 garlic cloves, crushed
3 cm (1¼ in) knob of ginger, finely grated
½ teaspoon salt
½ teaspoon freshly ground black pepper
2 teaspoons garam masala
1 teaspoon ground cumin
2 star anise
1½ cups (375 g) tomato passata (tomato purée)
1 cup (250 ml) thickened (heavy/pouring) cream

1. Preheat the oven to 180°C (350°F) fan-forced.
2. In a large bowl, combine the chicken, yoghurt, salt, pepper, garam masala, chilli powder and cumin. Set aside to marinate.
3. To make the butter chicken sauce, heat the butter over medium heat in a small saucepan. Add the onion, garlic, ginger, salt, pepper, garam masala, cumin and star anise and cook for 3–4 minutes, or until the onion has softened and the spices are fragrant.
4. Add the tomato passata and cream and cook for 5 minutes or until thickened slightly.
5. In a large baking dish, combine the rice with the stock and butter chicken sauce.
6. Add the chicken mixture and submerge. Cover with foil and bake for 45 minutes or until the rice is tender.
7. After 45 minutes, remove the foil and stir. Bake for a further 10 minutes until the edges have browned slightly. Sprinkle with chopped coriander to serve.

Storing instructions Allow to cool completely, then divide into individual portions and freeze in airtight containers for up to 2 months.

Leah's notes For something a little quicker and easier, you can use a store-bought butter chicken sauce instead of making your own.

Acknowledgements

I have so many people to thank for this book coming to life. Every single person has been an incredible help to me in one way or another, and I am so thankful for the team around me.

To my recipe testers: Mum, Cass, Desi and Eleanor, sorry for the ones that didn't work... oops! But thank you for all your helpful feedback in getting these recipes in tip-top shape with extra special spins on them.

Thank you Claudia and Lisa for editing my recipes from scribbles on paper to beautifully written whole recipes. Thank you for also being my recipe brain sounding boards, especially when I had serious baby brain in the kitchen!

Thank you to Murdoch Books for giving me the opportunity to create recipes for my community and for being so incredibly easy to work with. Vanessa and Cath – you both have brought this book to life in the most beautiful way.

And to my little family who support me in anything I do, I appreciate you more than you know. Mitch, you are the best husband and dad I could ask for, and without you by my side every day (even those early hours of the morning!), I couldn't have done this. Gigi and Jesse, this is for you my loves.

Index

C

D

E

F

G

H

K

L

M

Q

R

S

T

V

W

Y

Z

Published in 2026 by Murdoch Books, an imprint of Allen & Unwin

Murdoch Books Australia
Cammeraygal Country
83 Alexander Street
Crows Nest NSW 2065
Phone: +61 (0)2 8425 0100
murdochbooks.com.au
info@murdochbooks.com.au

Murdoch Books UK
Ormond House
26–27 Boswell Street
London WC1N 3JZ
Phone: +44 (0) 20 8785 5995
murdochbooks.co.uk
info@murdochbooks.co.uk

For corporate orders and custom publishing, contact our business development team at salesenquiries@murdochbooks.com.au

Publisher: Justin Wolfers
Editorial manager: Virginia Birch
Design manager: Kristy Allen
Designer and illustrator: Julia Cornelius
Editor: Yasmin Sabir
Photography: Cath Muscat/Rob Palmer
Stylist: Vanessa Austin
Home economist: Tammi Kwok
Production manager: Natalie Crouch

Murdoch Books acknowledges the Traditional Owners of the Country on which we live and work. We pay our respects to all Aboriginal and Torres Strait Islander Elders, past and present.

EU Authorised Representative: Easy Access System Europe, Mustamäe tee 50, 10621 Tallinn, Estonia, gpsr.requests@easproject.com

ISBN 978 1 76150 132 6

NATIONAL LIBRARY OF AUSTRALIA
A catalogue record for this book is available from the National Library of Australia

A catalogue record for this book is available from the British Library

Colour reproduction by Splitting Image Colour Studio Pty Ltd, Wantirna, Victoria
Printed in China by 1010 Printing International Limited

OVEN GUIDE: All the recipes in this book have been tested using a fan-forced (convection) oven. You may find cooking times vary depending on the oven and oven setting you are using. For conventional ovens, as a general rule, set the oven temperature to 20°C (25–50°F) higher than indicated in the recipe.

TABLESPOON MEASURES: We have used 20 ml (4 teaspoon) tablespoon measures. If you are using a 15 ml (3 teaspoon) tablespoon add an extra teaspoon of the ingredient for each tablespoon specified.

10 9 8 7 6 5 4 3 2 1

FSC www.fsc.org MIX Paper | Supporting responsible forestry FSC® C016973